"NEW NORMAL"

COVID-19 – TRANSFORMING INDIA

DR. MUKTA GOYAL

Contents

Preface

In different parts of the world, the educational system is facing some of its biggest trials yet, from the COVID-19 pandemic. The continuous closing of Schools and Colleges has vibrated the entire education system.

However, the ability of digital technologies to go beyond that has recently been revealed to the general public. Emerging technologies such as Artificial Intelligence (AI) aid in the development of vaccines, predicting which public health measures will be most effective, and keeping the public informed of scientific developments. They have also enabled us to move much of our lives online, keeping economic and educational systems running when most people are at home and keeping us connected to one another.

However, not all regions and social groups are equally capable of harnessing the power of digital technologies to combat the virus. This book focuses on how the pandemic serves as a widespread test case for the efficacy of these digital solutions, many of which will become permanent fixtures and cause long-term changes in many organisations. The innovations born of necessity may become long-lasting pillars of the organisations, allowing them to thrive long after the pandemic has passed. The coronavirus is forever changing the way we live and work.

This book helps to rehearse the Inner Work to areas of strength for construct wellness and to remain modest and adaptable, two credits basic to being a long lasting student.

Dr. Mukta Goyal

CHAPTER ONE

Effects of covid-19 on India's Digital Transformation

INTRODUCTION

In India, the standard of living is rising, and in order to meet the growing demands of Indian citizens, a large number of job opportunities must be created. Every year, the number of jobs required exceeds the number of job opportunities available in India. For a long time, India has focused primarily on its agricultural sector in order to improve its economic position. However, despite the availability of low-cost labour and fertile land, agricultural products are unable to contribute at the desired level. In light of these circumstances, the Prime Minister's decision to focus on the manufacturing sector is a noteworthy move. Since the beginning of the COVID-19 lockdown in late March, India has distributed around $5 billion in cash benefits to its most vulnerable citizens, entirely through digital payments.

• The Coronavirus accelerated the adoption of contactless digital technology in India.

• The digital-first reset has laid the groundwork for better governance, and Indian states are increasingly employing robots and drones.

According to data from India's apex Reserve Bank of India (RBI), the country now processes around 100 million digital transactions per day with a total value of 5 trillion rupees ($67 billion), a five-fold increase from 2016. The RBI anticipates a five-fold increase to 1.5 billion transactions per day worth 15 trillion rupees ($200 billion).

The United Payment Interface (UPI), a real-time payment system developed by the National Payments Corporation of India and overseen by the Reserve Bank of India, is at the heart of much of this.

Whether it's the use of Collaborative Robots (Co-Bot) by the government of Jharkhand or the municipal corporation of Bengaluru, India's tech hub, using drones to spray disinfectants, survey areas, monitor containment zones, and make public announcements, Indian states took advantage of the COVID-19 opportunity to further spread the use of technology.

Several other Indian states, including Telangana, Karnataka, and Gujarat, as well as cities like Varanasi, are taking similar steps to combat the pandemic's effects. State governments are also using technology to manage the demand for, availability of, and use of equipment such as ventilators, as well as essential medical items such as N95 masks and personal protective equipment (PPE).

Technology is bridging communities with local governments across cities and towns, decentralising decision-making. These innovative solutions, which make use of technology and digital tools, are having an impact on various aspects of life, including livelihoods, access to services, and education.

Make in India is a government of India initiative that encourages multinational and domestic companies to manufacture their products in India. Prime Minister Narendra Modi launched it on September 25, 2014. After the program's inception in 2015, India surpassed the United States of America and the People's Republic of China as the top global destination for foreign direct investment. Make in India is a campaign launched by Prime Minister Narendra Modi to assist all large business investors from around the world who want to do business in India. The PM launched this programme on September 25, 2014, at the Vigyan Bhawan in New Delhi. It is a significant step taken by the Indian government to reduce the level of unemployment among the country's youth.

Now is an excellent time to focus on digital transformation as the world considers ways to reduce the disruption caused to humanity.

This campaign was launched the day after the Mars mission, just before PM Modi's first visit to the United States as India's prime minister. The goal of launching this campaign in India is to make India a global manufacturing powerhouse, which will undoubtedly aid in resolving India's most pressing economic issue. This initiative was successfully launched in New Delhi with new deals for foreign investors, including Mukesh Ambani (Chairman of Reliance Industries), Azim Premji (Chairman of Wipro), and others.

- **Digital Transformation by Recognizing Its Necessities**

As the world is considering ways to reduce the disruption caused to humanity, now is an excellent opportunity to concentrate on digital transformation by recognizing its necessities:

- **Consumption of digital media**

The pandemic is driving digital transformation across corporate models, networks, and touchpoints, even if it is harmful to the economy. The need for increased organisational agility and deeper customer connections is at the heart of this transformation.

Prior to the outbreak of COVID-19, technology adoption and digital consumption had been rapidly increasing, with around 100 million people online. Despite the increase in coronavirus cases, the pandemic has accelerated the country's digital transformation, with the next 100 million consumers quickly moving online, effectively doubling the online market.

- **The Financial Sector's Digitalization**

The economy's foundational pillars, banking and payments, have seen a significant increase in digital offerings and adoption. In banking, digitalization is not a new concept, but the pandemic has accelerated the adoption of digital technologies with far-reaching implications for the financial sector's future.

As banks use technology to serve their clients and conduct routine operations, digitalization is playing a role.

- **Firms Recover Using Digital Technology**

According to a survey conducted by the IBM Institute for Business Value, COVID-19 has resulted in a 59 percent increase in digital transformation and a 66% belief that they can now execute activities that were previously difficult.

- **Digital Payments**

As a result of the viral outbreak, online grocery stores, small retail outlets, online pharmacies, and bill payments have all seen an increase in digital payments.

Contactless payments, such as those made with QR codes, wallets, UPI, or contactless cards, are gaining popularity because they offer convenience, security, and the ability to maintain social distance.

- **The use of technology is increasing.**

Whether it was the government of Jharkhand's use of Collaborative Robots (Co-Bot) or Bengaluru's municipal corporation using drones to spray disinfectants, survey areas, and make public announcements, Indian states took advantage of COVID-19 to further spread technology.

- **Growing Technology Use**

Indian states took advantage of COVID-19 to further spread technology, whether it was the government of Jharkhand's use of Collaborative Robots (Co-Bot) or Bengaluru's municipal corporation using drones to spray disinfectants, survey areas, and make public announcements.

- **Technology-driven strategy for the win**

This imperative has never been more important than it is now, thanks to the COVID-19 crisis. While strong leadership and alignment on overall strategy have long been indicators of success during disruptions or transformations, the extent to which technology plays a differentiating role in this crisis is striking.

During the crisis, executives at companies that experimented with new digital technologies and invested more capital in digital technology than their peers are twice as likely to report outsized revenue growth as executives at other companies. Nearly half of respondents at successful companies say they were the first to market with innovations during the crisis and that they were the first companies in their industries to experiment with new digital technologies. They are also more likely than others to report speeding up the time it takes for leaders to receive critical business information and reallocating resources to fund new initiatives. Both are key aspects of a culture of experimentation.

• The findings also show that, in addition to the multiyear acceleration of digital, the crisis has ushered in a paradigm shift in executive perspectives on the role of technology in business. Nearly half of executives ranked cost savings as one of their top priorities for their digital strategies in our 2017 survey. Only 10% of people think the same way about technology now; in fact, more than half say they're investing in technology to gain a competitive advantage or refocusing their entire business on digital technologies.

• Executives whose companies were losing money before the crisis are the most likely to adopt this mindset shift. Those who have seen the most revenue declines in recent years admit that they were behind their peers in their use of digital technologies—40 percent say so, compared to 24% at companies that have seen the most revenue growth—and also say that they have made far more significant changes to their strategies during the crisis than other executives report.

• Furthermore, respondents believe that technological capabilities are critical to success during a crisis. Talent, the use of cutting-edge technologies, and a variety of other capabilities are among the most significant differences between successful companies and all others. Having a culture that encourages experimentation and acting early is a related requirement for success.

Development, Digital, E-governance, Government, Internet access

Cloud computing and mobile applications are examples of digital technologies that have emerged as catalysts for rapid economic growth and citizen empowerment around the world. From retail stores to government offices, we are increasingly relying on digital technologies in our daily lives. They enable us to connect with one another and share information about issues and concerns that we face. By leveraging digital technologies, the Honourable Prime Minister hopes to transform our country and create opportunities for all citizens. Every citizen should have access to digital services, knowledge, and information, according to his vision. India is witnessing the next big thing: digital India. It aspires to profoundly affect the lives of everyone through transformation as it travels through rural and urban India.

The vision of Digital India initiative

The following diagram depicts the three visions: Here is what the Indian government hopes to achieve with its Digital India initiative.

• Infrastructure: The Digital India initiative aims to provide high-speed internet access to all Gram Panchayats' residents. At the individual level, bank accounts will be prioritised. In the country, people will have access to safe and secure cyberspace.

• Government services and governance: Citizens will have easy access to government services via the internet. Transactions will be simplified thanks to the use of electronic technology.

• Citizen digital empowerment: Providing universal digital literacy and making digital sources easily accessible is one of the most important aspects of the Digital India initiative. The services are also available.

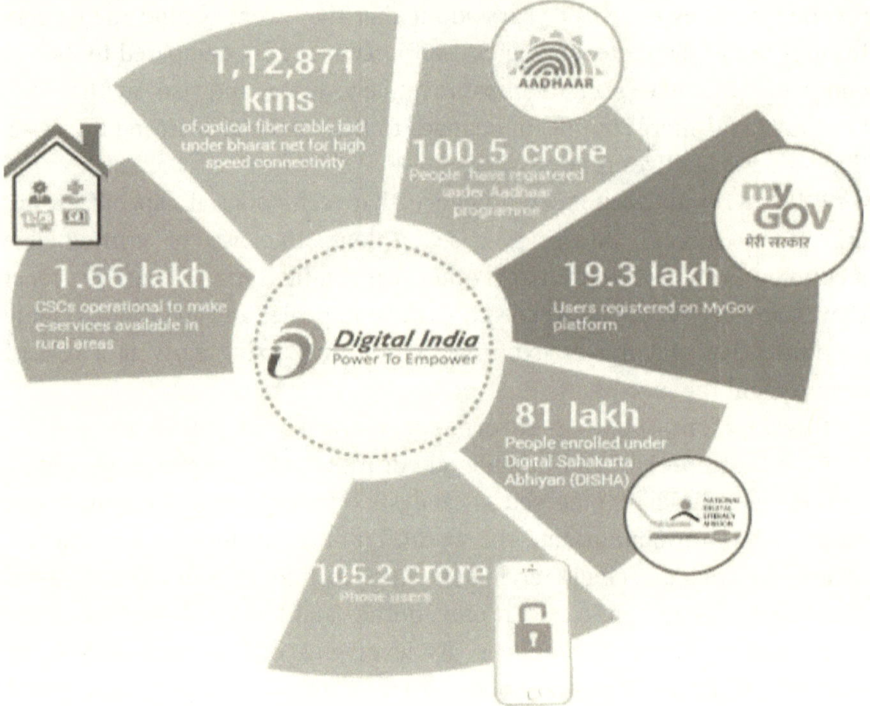

Source: adroitinfosystem.com

How Covid-19 is hastening the need for education's digital transformation Covid-19 pegged back India's education ambitions

India has made significant gains in education over the past decade, as the number of out-of-school children has decreased and enrolment at all education levels has risen overall. Covid-19, however, has disrupted this transformation, challenging the patterns and practices of India's education system and impacting the education of nearly 320 million students in the country. The digital evolution of education in India may seem inevitable, given that the nation is the world's second-largest internet market. Even before the pandemic, however, India had been experiencing concerning drop-out rates - a result of the disproportionate access to education. This problem has only grown progressively more serious during the pandemic due to the disparity in internet access. While we typically tend to associate this problem with more remote and poorer communities, less than half of urban households have trouble going online too.

Accelerating education's digitalisation

This is not to say that no efforts have been made to bridge the digital divide. State initiatives such as ePathshala, are helping to familiarise excluded communities with e-learning, providing educational online resources for educators as well as children and their parents.

More recently, the government also launched the PM eVIDYA programme as a way to broaden multi-mode access to digital education. The sudden disruptions caused by the pandemic, however, mean that long-term digitalisation efforts need to be supplemented with initiatives designed for the immediate recovery of India's education sector.

Some of BYJU's key features include elements of machine intelligence, such as the creation of Knowledge Graphs to personalise learning journeys based on each students' learning needs, as well as data analysis that helps make practice more engaging and in-depth.

Other Impacts of Digital India

The Digital India project provides a huge opportunity to use the latest technology to redefine the paradigms of service delivery. A digitally connected India can help in improving the social and economic condition of people living in rural areas through the development of non-agricultural economic activities apart from providing access to education, health and financial services. However, it is important to note that ICT alone cannot directly lead to the overall development of the nation. The overall growth and development can be realized through supporting and enhancing elements such as literacy, basic infrastructure, overall business environment, regulatory environment, etc.

Sustaining the new normal for India's education

As India emerges from the Covid-19 crisis, the future of education will still present challenges. The demand for digital transformation is not a short-term phenomenon, but rather an accelerating trend that the country and its education sector stakeholders are trying to make more ubiquitous.

Conclusion

The global effects of the Covid-19 pandemic have continued to be unprecedented. Lockdown measures have been implemented around the world to stem the spread of the virus, which has disrupted normal business and social activities. Countries have been forced to adapt to a "new normal" of living as a result of the emergency. "Make in India" was launched at a time when many countries around the world are expressing interest in doing business with India. The decision to launch the campaign at this time has greatly increased the campaign's chances of success. As a result, the manufacturing sector's contribution to GDP has increased as well.

With the help of technology and fast data, we certainly live in a world that is rapidly changing. While the internet is primarily used for entertainment and keeping in touch with friends for some, it has also provided new opportunities for growth and income for others. Businesses and government services have moved online, and in the years ahead, we can expect many more positive changes.

The Digital India programme is only the beginning of a digital revolution that, if properly implemented, will provide citizens with a plethora of new opportunities.

The Covid-19 pandemic has undoubtedly accelerated our progress toward self-sufficiency. We'll also have to make sure that these efforts help us move up the value chain. It is important to note that innovation will be a key enabler in our journey to attain self-reliance.

CHAPTER TWO

How Covid 19 can assist you in becoming smarter

Introduction:

The COVID-19 pandemic had a significant impact on many people around the world. Regular habits have shifted; even a simple stroll through the park is now viewed in a new light. The same is true for businesses. To accommodate, many organisations have closed or changed their social distance. During the first weeks of the crisis, new patterns of customer and employee behaviour and expectations emerged.

COVID-19 is a significant financial shock and burden. In recent weeks, the focus has shifted to ways to manage their health and safety threats while maintaining a reasonable level of business activity.

This scenario has been recently discussed and shares a corporate reaction to the pandemic. An increased awareness of risk will make customers more ready to pay for safety features, which in turn will provide greater motivation for manufacturers to develop and market innovations that meet consumer safety requirements.

In this process, businesses will re-evaluate their choices. It can invest in new as well as shelved innovations and product designs which are especially efficient in reducing risk and improving protection, even in cases where costs, usability and other quality measures are initially lower.

Importance of the Research

Companies have also been innovative in finding "low-hanging fruit" which can be rapidly incorporated in their activities during the pandemic. Grocery stores are adding Plexiglas shields at check-outs, restaurants and grocery stores have evolved to take-outs and supplies and video conferences in many industries.

Various critical and nonessential companies at the premises have introduced pre-bookings in China, both in terms of their outburst and the subsequent restart of the economy. They use wearable and software to monitor temperature-detection technology to identify customers at high risk for the virus in close real time.

Experiments in technology for risk reduction

Simultaneously, we're seeing companies develop and test far more radical risk-mitigation technologies. Developing new products and processes to reduce the risk of contagion is one of them. Robots have been designed to deliver medicines, meals, and collect bed sheets and trash in hospitals in China, for example. JD, the e-commerce behemoth, created a drone programme to deliver packages and spray disinfectant. Within a five-meter radius, smart helmets can detect anyone with a fever.

Other businesses, particularly those that do not use digital or automation technologies, have seen significant changes in their interactions with customers as a result of the crisis. Teachers transformed content and delivered it online or through phones in education, from elementary schools to universities.

The crisis has led to dramatic changes in their relationships with customers for other companies, especially those in which digital technology and automation are not widely used. Education transformed and distributed material, online and telephone, through teachers from elementary schools to universities. The Amazon Just Walk Out technology that integrates computer vision with IA has begun to license retailers to directly charge their customers as they are leaving the shop, without the need of check out. Many cultural industries, museums and galleries, movie theatres, concert halls, independent musicians and artists, have found ways to develop, perform and link to their audiences through online platforms.

Many managers now face one main question: how much and how much they invest in risk-measuring technology and corresponding product and services shifts. That depends to a large degree on how long the crisis lasts and what the danger (and fear) of contagion remains as soon as the summit is behind us. All of these factors will probably also differ widely among firms, markets and locations.

If there is a significant risk of contagion in the future there will be strong demand not just for contagion prevention, but also for long-term improvement in the behavior of customers and employees. In turn, this can lead to new demand. This has significant effects for consumers of technology, innovators, regulators and policy makers, both chances and obstacles.

Firms are forced to be smarter

Learning from forced innovation and investment in risk reduction technology will help businesses become intelligent and agile. For instance, businesses may have found spending time and money to experiment with remote work too expensive before the crisis. There were several solutions for the unfortunate COVID-19 crisis. Large call centers in China have invested heavily in IT equipment and systems to allow their employees to work from home and secure customer information. Our discussion with local managers around the country indicates that 20 to 40% of these staff in call centers have continued to operate remotely as these businesses begin to resume regular operations and that flexible home-work agreements will possibly become a permanent post-crisis strategy.

This forced exploration has resulted in a deeper knowledge of remote work in line with past studies. Workers who prefer home work can find improved productivity, decreased travel time and a lower rate of withdrawal, since they are happier overall. This expertise and investments in call centres have mitigated their reliability and information security issues for consumers during the crisis. The same applies even to business travel as businesses become intelligent in finding less responsive and interaction-critical voyages that can be replaced by teleconferencing.

Opportunities for market and reform

Just like the crisis has shown variations in employee expectations for homework, remote learning opportunities, entertainment and consumer behaviour would also influence consumer attitudes to digital and physical experiences. Valuable market opportunities can result in differences in customer preferences. The market will be stepped up for new digital goods, formats and content. It will accelerate investments in automation and digitalisation and create new goods, services and business models.

At the same time, some parts of the market will continue to support the physical experiences of the "old" model and to pay a premium for good quality, healthy physical consumption. Chances to compete (now enhanced) remote and digital alternatives may increase and distinguish physical offers.

There are also repercussions for policy makers for the growing need for risk reduction. The increased use of robotics, artificial intelligence and automation would challenge several countries' regulatory and liability frameworks. It would also impact employment, salaries and trade union negotiations. A wide use of temperature control and recording of the physical and health movement of people will contribute to privacy debates and data security discussions. These pressures ultimately create significant compromises and obstacles, but they also give policymakers valuable opportunities for innovation and learning.

In the midst of these tremendous interruptions, a mix of short and long-term solutions to technologies will give organisations a ray of hope. Innovative and innovative risk-mitigating solutions will contribute to improved consumer interactions and employee satisfaction now and in the future while the shorter term ultimately poses deep challenges for individuals and companies.

As the world comes out of the recession, workers will find innovative ways of communicating, entrepreneurs will take advantage of market opportunities previously unsustainable, administrators will be able to reassess innovation plans, customers are being able to use new environments, and policy and regulation will change to make everyone safer in the future. With foresight, the effects of these advances can also enable solutions to mitigate climate change (as travel has declined and virtual work infrastructures have expanded), to determine risks and to respond to emergencies in hazardous environments and broad-based biosafety, enabling our economic infrastructure to increase as it overcomes these difficult times.

Smart Cities: From a dream to reality

The government has set aside $1.2 billion to build 100 smart cities across the country. Think tanks, corporations, and government agencies are all working together to make this initiative a success.

While the entire country waits for this dream to come true, the question remains as to how close we are to seeing Smart Cities. What are the roadblocks? Mr Purushottam Kaushik, Managing Director- Sales, Leader-Growth Verticals, Cisco India & SAARC, spoke about the factors that will affect this Goa in an interactive webinar hosted by Economictimes.com and Cisco.

"Smart cities such as Agra, Chandigarh, Vadodara, Bengaluru, and Kakinada have been able to effectively tap technologies such as IoT/sensors, tele-healthcare, data, and analytics, and have contributed significantly to India's fight against COVID-19," says Sandeep Kolakotla, technology analyst at information analytics firm GlobalData. "Smart cities in India have been playing a major role and leading the way in the country's battle against the COVID-19 pandemic, as seen in many other countries around the world," he said. The success of smart cities has re-ignited interest in the project, which now has at least 100 smart cities in the works and a long road ahead of it.

The global health crisis definitely has helped to improve smart cities around the world. The pandemic has intensified enough what seemed a long-running dream. But when we come out of this pandemic, we must think carefully about the governance policies and the behavioural improvements that we must all make to ensure a healthier way to live in clever cities. Government agencies would also have to revise urban systems architecture in areas such as public transit, emergency response, and recreational facilities and so on, to help residents. City planners, technical companies and people will be involved partners in organising our future towns and, consequently, our lives. NXP helps cities worldwide to meet new levels of sustainability, performance, mobility and economic development by streamlined access to goods and services

.

City management equipped with IoT devices and a robust technology infrastructure can help to curb case transmission, while Ultra-Wide Band (UWB) technology is able to help people who are isolated to be tracked and monitored. In short, openness and trustworthy knowledge will help to build efficient eGovernance and effectively implement future cities, enabling people to trust the technology and government.

India's most powerful weapon in the fight against COVID-19 is smart cities.

Incorporating technologies

A Smart City's core tenet is built on not only easily accessible infrastructure but also technological advancements in government-citizen interaction. According to industry experts, the government's strategic deployment of technologies such as artificial intelligence, the internet of things, radio-frequency identification (RFID), and cloud computing has significantly reduced the country's resource deficit and empowered the government to do much more with much less.

A historic city with cutting-edge technology

The 3,000-year-old city of Varanasi is the perfect ambassador for the synthesis of age-old tradition with platforms and technologies of the twenty-first century, which is a hallmark of India's Smart Cities.

Cases of Covid-19 are being tracked.

Agra has also been collaborating with Gaia Smart Cities, an IoT startup, to use its technology platform to track COVID-19 cases, which includes a COVID-19 self-assessment app built on Microsoft Azure. Citizens can self-assess their health risk on the platform, which allows city officials to track responses via pin code and take preventive action. The gathered data also allows authorities to generate real-time reports, which aid in the monitoring of trends across the city.

"While it is too early to assess the level of success that India's smart cities have had in dealing with the current COVID-19 crisis, there is no doubt that they have led the country's fight back through innovative use of technology, paving the way for other cities to follow suit and become smarter," Kolakotla said.

COVID-19: How smart classrooms transform the education system of India

Outbreak of Coronavirus: The global pandemic has reached all parts of the economy massively. Although MNCs and professionals were marginally easier to adopt work as normal from home and continue to do business, the educational system around the world was overwhelming. Several academics, people, legislators and bureaucrats involved endorse the imagination and reinvention of the education system with disruptions throughout the board. So it comes with the intelligent systems in the classroom.

The implementation of intelligent school systems transforms the conventional education system. The sudden change is not only restricted to private schools but has also started to run smart classes in many government schools. While the crisis is crippling, technologically advanced are our schools and even universities. There should be no question that students and teachers had to change more than they had in the classrooms. In addition, many are not well equipped with remote learning technology.

"The use of education technology is one of the strategies which will help to increase education quality in India. The way education is delivered in India is also evolving. The present pandemic has improved the chances of developing infrastructure in the K12 and higher education sectors. Private schools have already got into e-learning bandwagons, smart classrooms and some even made pre-primary school tabs compulsory. Now, given the lockdown situation, you can expect that many EdTech companies will see and maybe take the opportunity to fill the void that might exist in the digital platform. As far as it may seem, virtual education will become the new standard for the next five years in India," said Teja Gudluru, the Founder and CEO of UDO-now.com.

"A crucial feature of the Covid-19 strategy is ensuring that the learning remains virtually an ongoing process. The new education transformation aimed at removing physical needs of teachers or classrooms by linking students and teachers using digital platforms and the required software through laptop or mobile devices. This is a perfect time for embracing the latest technologies and offers to improve the efficiency and productivity of student training through internet education and evaluation," said Kiran Dham, Globus Infocom AG's CEO.

Digital Transformation of Education System

Thanks to the rapid introduction of lock-down digital technologies, educational institutes, businesses, data processing approaches and strategies for online education have been pushed into tandem. Many educational institutions regard this as an ideal time to test and implement new technologies to allow and make education meaningful. Digital transformation has become a new standard with educational institutions around the country to escape the crisis hampering the curriculum. Many use this as an opportunity to be more productive and competitive while improving innovative and enhanced skills through online learning and evaluation.

The use of education technology has brought about an extraordinary change from teacher-centered education to student-centered education. Digital schools and numerous online platforms enable teachers and students to continue their interaction with the classroom style experience and to develop it. From teachers and parent reunions to employee / management meetings, smart classrooms provide all the interactivity needed.

"Technology transforms teacher-centered education from teaching to teacher-centered learning. Today, virtual courses and different online resources allow us to get the teacher and students involved as close as possible to a real experience in classroom. Tech-based curriculum increases the openness and equity of the education system. Digital education involves a fair coordination of course material, instructors, technologies and course users, and only with simple usable facilities such as internet connectors, on-line systems usability and affordability, PCs, tablets, apps and so on can it be implemented successfully. However, we cannot deny that COVID-19 has only accelerated technological adoption in these drastic circumstances to make quality education available to all."

Intervention by the Government

The central Government, state governments and private players have come up with various initiatives to help and benefit students in response to the challenge that colleges and schools face. Since the lock-up began, the government has taken several steps to ensure that the crisis has the least impact on education. Various e-learning portals and applications were introduced by public authorities and education organizations such as the DIKSHA portal, the e-Swayam, the STEM focused games, etc. to help students continue their learning during the pandemic.

Summing It All Up

The online evaluation sites or technology companies aim to develop their products continuously. Much was planned and introduced and there has been further progress

The huge use of technology in teaching in the sense of crises would lead to a new age in the education field, in which students will benefit from the best of the faculty worldwide. In future, significant criteria are the quality of the faculty, the quality of IT infrastructure and the acquaintance with digital teaching technologies. The crisis has, without doubt, accelerated the adoption of education technology and will help to improve the digital learning infrastructure of the countries on a long-term basis.

"It will last years, if not more, the effects of COVID-19. The new normal is for considerably more students to take lessons from home. Although this trend has now gone up, COVID-19 will give it a big boost. The best thing is that India is able to teach students lakhs at home. The nation has one of the biggest 4G networks in the world. 4G access is accessible in virtually every part of the world. The fact that data are very inexpensive is even more impressive. Classes can be easily streamed across such robust networks. Students who learn in virtual classes will discover that they have as well or maybe even better learning experience than students who are in class. The enormous disruptive force of virtual classrooms is the opportunity to offer endless courses at the doorstep of the students. A student living in the interior can take an AI or Big Data course without paying a substantial fee. The number of students who have earned an education online in the next few years will also increase significantly," said Diwakar Chittora, the IntelliPaat Founder and CEO.

Artificial intelligence is paving the way for the transformation of cities into smarter and more productive working and living areas. Cities are now witnessing a, some would argue long overdue, transformation in the way they are organised, controlled and manoeuvred, caused by the pandemic. City life is adjusting to a new standard, from socially distanced walkways to reduced public transport use. The way and time they go to work are changing for commuters, buses are reducing their capacity and operation, and more cyclists are taking to the road.

- Technology driving the revolution

Technology is crucial in order for cities to handle these changes. In order to remain integrated and to communicate concerns and ideas, a smart city needs a vast range of technology operating in tandem with each other. In terms of transport specifically, the evolution of the smart city revolves around three main areas: better road data, real-time control systems for existing infrastructure, and the potential intersection of infrastructure with vehicle and fleet technologies.

Covid-19 has also seen travel patterns becoming less predictable, and AI sensors can help to regulate traffic signals, track traffic flow, and provide anonymous numerical data in determining active travel routes for cyclists and pedestrians with the end of rush hour possibly becoming a reality. All these things are achieved by a completely working 'intelligent junction' in one. A new 5G network will enable this, and will be central to the next step of the smart city and IoT, allowing more connected sensors and faster processing of larger cloud datasets.

- The future is now happening.

Covid-19 is certainly proving to be a catalyst for improvement. The future is arriving faster and technology offers the means to shape it. With less waiting time and more smooth traffic flow, we would expect journeys to become greener, more integrated. City facilities for healthy travel, flexible pedestrian-only zones and cycling paths, and public transit networks that can respond to changing crowd-flow peaks.

Cities are now being immediately reactive to the movement around them using AI and other technologies, working towards a holistic and anonymous technology and city zones ecosystem, allowing all modes of transport and movement to navigate their way through the ever-changing metropolis.

Conclusion:

The pandemic has pushed organizations around sectors to think of new solutions for work. Although COVID-19 was a crisis of unprecedented proportions and rightly made us doubt existing work practices, it will now be our duty to look at the future with hope and the confidence that the economy of the country can bounce back. Via WFH, workers around the world have continued to perform their activities remotely, thanks largely to the digital networks that exist in the world today. However, WFH is not a viable job-style, as this paper has argued, and instead the industry shows a decided pivot towards a 'work from anywhere' model. The hope is that the government, businesses and employees will coalesce around the principle of working remotely.

The accelerated remote work culture born during COVID-19 is bound to further boost the growth of flexible workspaces, particularly as many employers view remote work as a long-term practice. To manage this development and to ensure that the economy benefits from our creative workplace solution, a symbiotic and sustained partnership between the government and the flexible workspace industry is required (s).

In the years to come, 24 March 2020 will always be seen as the day India came to a standstill. But if history tells us one thing, it is that times of crisis may turn into opportunities. Looking back, the aftermath of China's SARS outbreak persuaded millions of Chinese customers to embrace a network called Alibaba, while the Y2K bug turned into a veiled blessing for the Indian IT industry and increased the outsourcing of business processes.

CHAPTER THREE

In the Wake of the Covid-19 Pandemic, an E-Learning Initiative

Introduction

Corona Virus, also known as Covid-19, is a deadly and infectious disease that has had a significant impact on the global economy. This tragedy has also shaken the education sector, and this fear is likely to spread throughout the world's education sector. Many schools and colleges were forced to close temporarily due to the Covid-19 pandemic. Several areas are affected globally, and there is concern that the current semester, as well as future semesters, will be lost. In-person instruction has been phased out at a number of schools, colleges, and universities. According to the researchers, it is unlikely that normal teaching will resume anytime soon. Because social distancing is so prevalent at this point, learning opportunities will suffer as a result.Covid-19 has changed our lives drastically. It has not just impacted our physical health but has affected global mental health. The pandemic has changed our way of doing work, interacting with others while maintaining safe social distance, and especially impacted the learning process of students. It resulted in the shutting down of schools all over the world. 1.2 billion

Educational institutions are scrambling to come up with solutions to this difficult situation. These circumstances highlight the importance of scenario planning for academic institutions (Rieley, 2020). This is a situation that necessitates humanity and cooperation. Our students, faculty, academic staff, communities, societies, and the country as a whole all need to be protected and saved.

Students no longer have classrooms, globally. Keeping this in mind, Education Ministry has released the New Education Policy (NEP) in 2020, seeing the growing need for an online platform for education in India. Although the whole world has stopped it's essential to find alternatives to keep going. Online education platforms are one of a kind. BYJU'S, an Indian, Bangalore-based e-learning start-up has become the world's most valuable e-learning company. They have announced free classes as well, which increased their productivity by 200%.

Importance of online education in the current scenario

Although we faced a sudden change and it's clearly hard to adjust, especially when it isn't a choice or our preference. The change happened in no moment of time that it didn't allow us to get prepared or used to it. However, this sudden change helped us to live in such difficult times and continued with our work. Online education is an effective initiative to let students continue with studies without any gap.

Here are some benefits of online education jotted down below:

Cost-effective

EdTech has been considered more effective in terms of cost. Courses available online are more cost-friendly. Parents can save the cost of traveling from home to school. Students can engage their time more on learning than traveling.

Flexible

In school, the timings are fixed, and schedules are set, and students have to work accordingly. It gets hectic of students to be at schools for start 5-6 hrs, with only 1hr break. With the use of new technology, everything can be found online, and it saves time. Classes timings are even more flexible now.

Better visualization

Learning is accelerated when we use words to create mental images. However, if was seen that visualized learning helps students to grasp information more quickly.

Automatic approach

As education application platforms are automatic, it helps prevent human-made errors. Putting and rearranging data and all the information has become a lot easier.

Less paperwork

While looking at the environmental ways, using education technology reduces the use of paper. Students have started making notes on computers and assignments are submitted in PDF formats.

Stress associated with EdTech

As an increasing number of countries apply lockdown in response to coronavirus, our social lives have changed drastically. It isn't surprising that the mental health of everyone has taken a dive throughout the pandemic. During the lockdown, the idea of distance learning became widely popular and has been applied the same by schools and universities globally. This transition of online classes has impacted teachers, students, and their parents.

Visual learning has significantly increased the time students spend on devices. The increased usage of screen time has been found to be highly linked with increased depression, stress, anxiety, and perceived attention problems. Another major issue is the altered sleep cycle of students. Students studying in international universities face difficulty because of different time zones, and they have to adjust their time accordingly. This affects their regular sleep pattern and eventually hampers the circadian rhythm and biological clock. Increased screen time also resulted in disturbed circadian rhythm. These are the reasons which increase problems like headache, ineffective time management, fatigue, lack of motivation, feeling of loneliness, procrastination among students.

Online classes not only disturb mental health conditions but also has a great impact on the physical health of students. A set routine helps an individual to live a better lifestyle, but because of online classes, students don't have any set routine to follow. They sit in front of their laptops or computers for hours without walking between classes. As this transition imposed many challenges, it is advised to be physically active and eat healthy for better health. Students are advised to practice self-care, self-compassion, and forgiveness for better mental health. Take a break in between classes, observe your surroundings, and then proceed.

Other helpful ideas to improve mental health and well-being are doing yoga, meditation, drawing, listening to music, doing anything you like and feel therapeutic, staying organized, cleaning your space, and if needed, seeking professional help.

Reccomendations

Most education systems have been forced to adopt alternatives to face-to-face teaching and learning as a result of the current COVID-19 crisis. Many educational systems moved activities online to ensure that instruction could continue even if schools were closed.

When compared to the alternative of not going to school, online learning has proven to be a valuable tool for continuing to develop skills during school closures. However, there are still concerns that online learning may have been a sub-optimal substitute for face-to-face instruction, particularly in the absence of universal access to infrastructure (hardware and software) and inadequate teacher and student preparation for the unique demands of online teaching and learning.

Students can overcome some of the potential challenges posed by online learning by developing strong attitudes toward learning, such as remaining focused during online classes or maintaining sufficient motivation. They are also critical in assisting students in effectively using information and communication technology (ICT) and making the most of new learning technologies. Positive learning attitudes, self-regulation, and intrinsic motivation to learn all play a role in improving school performance, but they may be especially important if online learning continues.

The support students receive from their families and teachers, as well as the role models they are exposed to, have a significant impact on their attitudes and dispositions. rning atmosphere Providing support for teacher training in the use of digital resources for pedagogical purposes.

Different types of family and teacher support, such as parental emotional support and teacher enthusiasm, have been found to be important for the development of positive learning attitudes and can ensure that students acquire the attitudes and dispositions that will allow them to maximise their ability to take advantage of online learning opportunities. However, due to a lack of time, insufficient digital skills, or a lack of curricular guidelines, some families and teachers may find it difficult to provide such support, particularly during the COVID-19 crisis.

In order to improve information and guidance to parents on effective practises for supporting their children's learning, education systems should strive to strengthen engagement between schools and parents. Teachers, on the other hand, require assistance in incorporating technology effectively into their teaching practises and methods, as well as in assisting students in overcoming some of the challenges that come with this type of learning environment. To ensure that ICT is effectively leveraged, it is critical to support teachers' training in the use of digital resources for pedagogical practise and to promote teaching practises that are adapted to this context.

Conclusions

To stop the spread of the COVID-19 virus, many countries have had to close schools, colleges, and universities. Because of the long-term negative effects of school closures on skill accumulation, many educational systems have moved online at an unprecedented rate. Because lockdowns may be implemented again in the future until effective vaccines or therapeutics are available, governments must reflect on the major challenges that students, parents, teachers, and school principals have faced in adapting to this phase of massive online learning and intervene to better harness the potential of online learning.

They should, for example, first expand infrastructure to ensure that no one is left out of online classes, and then support students and teachers in effectively using online tools and technologies.

This policy brief illustrates how students' attitudes and dispositions toward learning, such as ambition or motivation, are important drivers of their educational achievements and can help ensure that online learning is as effective as possible, based on forthcoming analysis in the Skills Outlook 2021. Furthermore, this brief demonstrated that both families and teachers play critical roles in guiding children through the challenges of home learning: parents can provide emotional and educational support to their children, while teachers can act as mentors, encouraging active learning and motivation while ensuring that no one falls behind.

Such interventions can significantly improve the effectiveness of online learning. Given the critical role that families and teachers play in school closures, governments can help them engage more effectively by expanding family leave opportunities and improving school-parent communication, for example.

CHAPTER FOUR

Covid -19:India's Entrepreneurship Challenges and Opportunities

Introduction

How business owners reacted to the pandemic

Entrepreneurs are known for their flexibility, which was demonstrated during the Covid-19 pandemic: 73% of the time of entrepreneurs polled revised their business plans (By mid-March, two out of every three had done so.) almost three-quarters of Many entrepreneurs applied for government assistance. Almost half of the entrepreneurs were successful in attracting new customers. By developing business opportunities during the lockdown of new items and services (especially in the digital space), Others examined their business practices or repositioned themselves. completely different businesses Many entrepreneurs used existing resources. Others began to cater for the digital and online capabilities; healthcare industry (NHS/Covid) given the interdependence of entrepreneurs and their businesses, The impact of the pandemic on their businesses Entrepreneurs' mental health their happiness in life.

During the crisis, perceived stress increased. Many entrepreneurs began working from home over time. two out of every three people work solely or primarily from home. In conjunction with childcare (due to school and other obligations), Due to the closure of nurseries, this added stress to more than one in every five children. among the respondents Despite the fact that most people's primary concern is the survival of their business was at stake, two out of every three people contributed personal funds, and one one-third volunteered their personal time, and 44% a number of entrepreneurs volunteered their company's services/products for charitable purposes (assisting other businesses, charities, or the general public) workers). Almost half did so as a result of the pandemic. Long-term opportunities and constraints With confidence, entrepreneurs looked to the future. Almost half believe their company will survive the crisis. and One-third expects their company to be even bigger than it is now. pre-pandemic. 72.5 per cent of entrepreneurs expect to grow their businesses. Over the next five years, they plan to add employees to their company. Past According to research, such expectations are a good predictor of job creation over time Entrepreneurs also expected acceleration of their existing businesses business, frequently linked to online services Many people anticipate a cost.

Entrepreneurs must adapt to a new environment in the wake of the worldwide COVID-19 pandemic. Entrepreneurs must demonstrate risk-taking and innovative abilities in order to combat the epidemic. They will also need to use various action plans as a business founder, in various locations based on their sector and industry.

On May 12, 2020, the Ministry of Finance announced a special economic package called the 'Atma Nirbhar Bharat Abhiyan' or 'Self Reliant India' mission to combat the COVID-19 pandemic in India. The Indian government took necessary steps to help existing micro, small, and medium-sized businesses, as well as new entrepreneurs to emerge.

The finance minister announced the first tranche of the 'Atma Nirbhar Bharath Abhiyan', which will assist existing micro, small, and medium businesses. It provides financial assistance to existing businesses in order for them to survive. It rewrote the definition of a micro, small, and medium-sized enterprise (MSME). The distinction between manufacturing and service sectors must be eliminated. Amendments to the law will be enacted.

The Indian government has launched a number of initiatives to encourage new business ventures. The schemes offer financial assistance and guidance to entrepreneurs with COVID -19 pandemic solutions. The Startup India scheme is putting resources forward with a variety of partners. Startups will be promoted by stakeholders. They guide entrepreneurs by hosting webinars and providing information and resources to help them get off to a good start in these unprecedented times.

Discussion

Entrepreneurship Challenges During Covid-19

The following are the challenges that entrepreneurs faced during the COVID-19 period:

- **Lockdown Issues**

As a result of the nationwide lockdown, businesses of all sizes are feeling the effects and being forced to rethink how they manage and operate their operations, including revisiting their business plans. Problems such as social isolation and travel restriction, employment barriers, and a changing environment all had an impact on entrepreneurship.

- **Operational Barriers**

With social distancing becoming the norm, businesses that had to postpone their physical operations shifted their operations online and implemented work-from-home policies (WFH). The physical activities of the businesses must be shifted to a new platform.

- **Decline in Sales**

The decrease in firm sales during the lockdown period had a negative impact on enterprise operations and revenue. Customers purchased products based on their priorities. Those businesses that face insufficient delivery mechanisms face sales barriers. A drop in sales results in a drop in business revenue.

- **Difficulty in Meeting Working Capital**

Because of the decline in revenue, it is difficult to make short-term payments. Payments to creditors, bills, and current liabilities cannot be met within the time frame specified.

- **Personnel Management**

There was a situation in which not all employees were able to come to work. Employees who are sick are not permitted to come to work. Some of them will be quarantined, and the areas will be designated as containment zones. Employees who are quarantined are only permitted to return to work if they are not infected with the disease. As a result, businesses had to deal with the issue of employee management. This had a negative impact on the company's operations.

- **Innovation**

Entrepreneurs in this situation will need to use innovation to overcome the new challenges they face. Entrepreneurs must devise new ways to deal with the current crisis.

- **Digital Environment**

As the COVID-19 pandemic continues to disrupt supply chain processes and businesses around the world, consumer shopping habits have shifted, forcing many businesses to shift to online channels in order to maintain sales. Entrepreneurs must convert their businesses to digital platforms. Enterprises must reconsider their digitization strategy and implement measures to ensure long-term viability in order to face the longer-term challenges.

- **Availability of Capital**

Due to the changing environment caused by COVID-19, new entrepreneurs faced the problem of lack of capital for their business. The lack of economic activity during the lockdown period makes it difficult to raise capital for new businesses.

- **Marketing Strategy**

Existing marketing strategies may fail to deliver the product to customers in time for COVID-19. Marketing strategies should be adjusted in response to changing circumstances. Adopt marketing strategies that maximise return on investment through efficient, targeted advertising. marketing that produces results.

Entrepreneurship Opportunities

Indian entrepreneurship opportunities in the existing MSME sector during COVID-19:

Assistance To The Msme Sector

The Indian MSME sector is the backbone of the economy. It accounts for 30% of Gross Domestic Product (GDP), with MSME exports accounting for 48%. It is the second-largest employer after agriculture. It employs 110 million people in India.

Atma Nirbhar Bharath Abhiyan's Assistance

The Atma Nirbhar Bharath Abhiyan intends to meet the needs of MSMEs by providing various forms of financial assistance. In addition, the government has completed the distinction between manufacturing and service-related MSMEs and expanded the scope of micro, small, and medium-sized enterprises.

Other MSMEs Interventions

- Because of COVID, MSMEs are currently experiencing marketing and liquidity issues.
- E-market linkage for MSMEs will be promoted as a replacement for trade fairs and exhibitions.
- Using data generated by the e-marketplace, fintech will be used to improve transaction-based lending.
- The government has continuously monitored the payment of dues to MSME vendors by the government and Central Public Sector Undertakings.
- MSME receivables from the government and central public sector enterprises (CPSEs) are to be released in 45 days.

Impact Of Covid-19 On Entrepreneurship

COVID-19 has been followed by social distancing, and the lockdown has had a significant impact on the business market. Entrepreneurs anticipate how they will manage and operate their businesses in order to keep the financial wheel turning. The market has changed as a result of COVID-19. Businesses needed to rethink their approach to entrepreneurship. The transition to working from home has produced positive results, as it has ensured business continuity at a low cost while also improving quality and productivity in most organisations. Industries such as healthcare, education, entertainment, and basic necessities are thriving. The simulated stimulation results in the physical existence of systems online.

The Indian government has proposed a number of schemes to assist existing MSMEs and new startups in overcoming the barriers imposed by COVID-19. The Ministry of Finance announced a series of relief measures, including tax and other corporate exemptions, regulatory compliances, in order to reduce the compliance burden on MSMEs during COVID-19.

Conclusion

As COVID-19 expands, the livelihoods of many entrepreneurs and small businesses are jeopardised. Entrepreneurs face numerous challenges, such as dealing with short-term challenges, lowering barriers to entrepreneurship, and increasing entrepreneurial potential to help accelerate growth. In the long run, the recovery will protect overall employment.

This can be accomplished through activities that keep startups active in the short term while also increasing the growth potential of new firms.

Supply chains have been significantly disrupted and reduced as a result of the lockdown, as much as supply and demand for labour. COVID-19 is a test for both existing and new businesses. For entrepreneurs, crisis periods present both a challenge and new opportunities. Startups are able to overcome obstacles such as difficult health or financial situation, as well as respond to shifting priorities and needs.

As entrepreneurs face challenges, they must view the current economic downturn as an opportunity to develop new ideas. The government develops plans to promote existing MSMEs and entrepreneurship in order to address the COVID-19 challenges in health care and social services, safeguards and barriers. Raise awareness of current guidelines and provide support for initiatives to assist entrepreneurs in dealing with the COVID-19 crisis.

CHAPTER FIVE

Coping Adaptability and Mental Health Concerns in the "New Normal"

Introduction

Our daily routines and "business as usual" mentality were disrupted by the COVID-19 pandemic, which resulted in the need for numerous adjustments in both our personal and professional lives. These changes had an effect on us mental, physical, and emotional. Today, we'll talk about and investigate how to successfully exit the pandemic and establish new habits while creating a new routine normal for us, our families, and the people we assist. Our goal is to discuss the pandemic's lasting effects on healthcare professionals as also investigate constructive coping and management techniques.

The pandemic has set off a variety of passionate, physical, and monetary issues however amidst this emergency, countries have shared and gained from one another's encounters.

The COVID-19 pandemic has made millions stay at home or seriously confine their exercises. This significant interruption expands the gamble for gloom and tension. When outside powers lessen our capacity to control our lives, it is essential to zero in on those things we CAN handle. This study is making a stock of contemplations and exercises that individuals all around the world have appraised as far as supportiveness in excess sincerely solid.

"Certain individuals might have incidental concerns that are contained to specific parts of their life, or might be time-restricted

Assembling Again: How to Do So Safely

A warm climate and a higher level of inoculated individuals imply expanded movement, which can cause worry for individual wellbeing. For the individuals who feel some tension in social occasion again with individuals, Dr. Youn has a few hints:

- **Begin slow:** If you realize that in a month's time you'll start associating with bigger gatherings, meet with one individual now and gradually develop your circle. Follow all COVID security conventions like removing and wearing veils, however, start associating with individuals at a speed that is ideal for you to assist with decreasing tension
- **Know and keep up with limits:** Friends and family might have different solace levels with unexpected exercises in comparison to you might have. In these cases, it is vital to know your limits and obviously convey them. These limits might move contingent upon the circumstance and relationship, yet the expectation is that you are with individuals who will comprehend and come to a settlement on security

Do you recall this image that got out and about via web-based media toward the beginning of lockdown? The one that basically said: "Your grandparents were called to war, you're being called to sit on your lounge chair. You can do this." While it was intended to lift our spirits, nobody knew at the time that the world was managing one of the best long-haul dangers confronting mankind.

Characteristics and Signs of a Traumatized Person

- Shock, denial, or disbelief Confusion, trouble concentrating Anger, irritability, mood swings Anxiety and fear Guilt, shame, and self-blame Withdrawing from others Feeling depressed or hopeless Feeling disconnected or numb
- Compassion fatigue is characterised by the following characteristics and symptoms: chronic physical and emotional exhaustion; depersonalization; feelings of unfairness toward the therapeutic or caregiver relationship; irritability; feelings of self-contempt; difficulty sleeping; weight loss; headaches; and the point at which "flatten the curve" feels more like "iron the mountain."

What is the post-pandemic pressure problem?

Over a year after the fact and with just about 4,000,000 lives lost, we are a long ways from ordinary. Indeed, as indicated by the World Health Organization, the COVID-19 pandemic has caused more 'mass injury' for a bigger scope than the subsequent universal conflict and the emotional well-being cost of the Covid pandemic will endure "for a long time to come". This injury is what a few clinical experts are calling a post-pandemic pressure issue, a type of COVID-19-instigated PTSD. While PPSD isn't (yet) a perceived emotional well-being condition, specialists unequivocally accept it ought to be. The Post-pandemic pressure problem isn't yet an authority term. However, it was begotten by psychotherapist Owen O'Kane as an approach to portraying the psychological effect of living through the pandemic.

As per O'Kane, manifestations of PPSD are like those of post-horrible pressure issues (PTSD).

They can shift from one individual to another, yet can include:
• Expanded uneasiness.
• Sensations of sadness.
• Low inspiration.
• Feeling wild.
• Disturbed rest.
• Expanded or diminished hunger.
• Feeling numb.
• Pulling out from social circumstances.
• Being effortlessly unsettled.
• Disastrous reasoning and envisioning awful.

O'Kane says that individuals with existing psychological instabilities could be more powerless to PPSD, and their manifestations may be more serious.

"In the event that you have recently experienced uneasiness or gloom, the indications might be more terrible. Assuming you were working admirably before the pandemic and are currently encountering these side effects, it is possible you are encountering PPSD," he says.

He focuses on the significance of looking for help assuming you experience these side effects and they happen routinely. Assuming your awful days dwarf your great days, you should create a GP arrangement and they can offer assistance, like treatment or prescription.

The pandemic has been a difficult valuable encounter for the vast majority, so there isn't any disgrace in requesting some psychological help.

There is dependably assist with excursion there assuming that you've persevered through a horrendous life occasion.

In the interim, **Dr. Dan Chisholm,** an emotional well-being expert for the WHO in Copenhagen, **Denmark, says:** "Coronavirus has had various consequences for individuals' psychological wellness and prosperity, going from stresses over becoming contaminated, or the pressure achieved by disease avoidance and lockdown, self-seclusion and quarantine, or the negative impact on psychological well-being related with lost positions, pay, instruction or mingling."

"The combined impact of these actions has prompted expansions in pressure and nervousness, as well as gloom and dejection," he adds. "For some, the indications related with these circumstances will reduce as the general wellbeing circumstance improves and limitations are facilitated, however for other people, the experience of having had Covid-19, or living through the pandemic will have dependable impacts, specifically for cutting edge medical services laborers or dispossessed relatives."

One additionally needs to consider youngsters and youths, who, **as Andrea Raballo,** academic partner of psychiatry at the University of Perugia in Italy, brings up have been presented to "conceivably undermining features of the pandemic in such fragile progress years," the impacts of which "actually must be appropriately valued and perceived, since the impacts could arise on schedule."

Dublin-based Eliana Colantonio, 30, was determined to have PTSD recently subsequent to experiencing an extreme instance of Covid-19 on vacation leave in Italy last October. "I was apprehensive I planned to quit breathing and would bite the dust alone, away from my loved ones back home in Argentina." Her horrifying aggravation endured 20 days until she improved, yet obviously, she was damaged by the experience, prompting fears of getting it again and not having the option to endure it a subsequent time.

Step by step instructions to adapt to PPSD

The impacts of any injury can be weakening, however, there are ways of overseeing them. **Sundas Pasha,** a California-based clinical therapist, says that throughout the most recent year she has seen an expansion in the number of individuals both looking for and offering mental help comparable to pandemic-related injury.

"Since it's a more up-to-date subset of injury, individuals are searching for ways of holding and backing each other through these questionable times, and

for the times ahead. It's been extraordinary to see individuals meeting up and sharing assets and data for those battling."

She strongly suggests treatment as an asset.

"A ton of experts have been equipped with survival techniques and procedures to help those managing the consequence and impacts of the pandemic. We are quite far from conquering the emotional wellness effect of this previous year, yet having a spot to discuss it and take care of through any problems or battles is an extraordinary method for refocusing."

Meanwhile, O'Kane recommends mental conduct treatment (CBT) - broadly utilized for PTSD, nervousness, and despondency certain drugs, workout schedules, and care groups.

There are a few stages you can take to rehearse pressure the board:

- **Get normal exercise** - practice diminishes your body's development of the pressuring chemical, cortisol. It additionally delivers endorphins, which are synthetics that cause you to feel better. You should find exercises that you appreciate and tenderly simplify yourself into an exercise routine. Try not to propel yourself, notwithstanding, and counsel your GP prior to participating in any difficult active work to guarantee it is ok for you.

- **Practice yoga** - in the event that activity isn't for you, yoga can be a more delicate approach to dealing with your feelings of anxiety. It assists with loosening up your body and quieting your brain, as well as giving incredible exercise to your heart. Yoga can bring down your circulatory strain and your gamble of creating coronary illness. It likewise helps when you simply need a break, away from the stressors of regular day-to-day existence.

- **Inhale profoundly** - rehearsing profound breathing activities can be a gainful approach to battling pressure. Unwinding practices assist with bringing more oxygen into your body and have been displayed to diminish circulatory strain levels and stress chemicals.

- **Get a lot of rest** - having a strong design around your rest is significant for facilitating pressure. Coordinate a reasonable sleep time routine and permit yourself to loosen up prior to hitting the sack. Attempt to get 7-9 hours of rest every night where conceivable.

- **Associate** - investing energy with individuals you love can be so great for your psychological well-being. One investigation really discovered that investing energy with companions and youngsters assists with delivering the normal pressure calming synthetic, oxytocin. Many examinations have additionally proposed that individuals with a solid companionship bunch will generally live longer and recuperate better after awful wellbeing occasions, for example, a respiratory failure. Having individuals near you to incline toward likewise implies you can offload your pressure, and talk concerning what is annoying you.

- **Put down stopping points** - notwithstanding, figuring out how to say no can be a friend in need for the people who battle with pressure. In the event that you're battling to stay aware of the hurrying around of regular daily existence, it very well may be savvy to sit out of friendly plans and reserve time for yourself. Your companions and family members will comprehend assuming that you want a break. Plan for time for yourself, as well concerning others, rather than attempting to be wherever with everybody, constantly.

Source: annualreviews.org

Discussion and Findings

For some, a re-visitation of "typical" could mean tending to psychological wellness challenges that strengthened or emerged during the pandemic. We have heard from numerous local area individuals regarding how their emotional well-being manifestations have expanded during the pandemic; others have encountered psychological wellness conditions, including gloom and tension, interestingly. Assuming that you have a specialist as well as a therapist, keep on discussing how you are doing. Assuming you have as of late evolved pressure and additionally end up confronting new psychological wellness challenges, check in with your essential consideration specialist and examine how you are feeling. As usual, connect with your organization for help and look for help in the event that you really want it. There is help and trust.

1. **Recognize and address your psychological well-being difficulties.**

We know from overviews and studies that the pandemic has affected our aggregate social wellbeing. A review directed in June 2020 uncovered that "40.9% of respondents revealed something like one antagonistic mental or social medical issue, including indications of uneasiness problem or burdensome issue (30.9%), manifestations of an injury and stressor-related turmoil (TSRD) connected with the pandemic (26.3%), and having begun or expanded substance use to adapt to pressure or feelings connected with COVID-19 (13.3%)."

1. **Observe and acknowledge how you feel :** Whenever you are worried, unfortunate, or awkward, interruption to ponder what you are feeling and think about the thing is initiating those sentiments. Perhaps conversing with a companion about plans to head out to the films is making your stomach fix, looking on the web so that flights might be able to see family after over a year is blowing your mind, or considering a re-visitation of the workplace is making you need to hit rest on the caution for a fourth time frame. Whenever you perceive how you are feeling and what is making you feel off-kilter or focused, you can delay having some time off and investigate what's happening. Without judgment, you can zero in on ways of tending to what you're feeling and plan for what comes straightaway.

2. **Go at your own speed and put down your own stopping points:** Acknowledge how you feel and settle on choices that vibe ideal for you. Begin with being straightforward with yourself about your cutoff points, and don't feel awful on the off chance that you're not prepared to continue face-to-face or public exercises.

3. **Be direct with regard to what works for you:** Have a go at being immediate while talking about plans with loved ones. Not prepared for ordinary mingling? Have a go at utilizing "I" proclamations so obviously, you are settling on choices in light of your own requirements: "I'm not prepared for that at the present time" or "I can't make it this time, however, the trust we can soon." Being forthright can likewise reassure others. Keep in mind, we've all be affected by the pandemic.

4. **Practice care:** Whenever you're anxious, reflecting could appear to be unimaginable, but we realize it can work. Begin delayed with taking in a quiet area, or sitting outside with some tea (without looking through your telephone!). Profound breathing, contemplation, and careful practices can prepare our mind to all the more likely oversee pressure. Assuming that you are new to care, consider applications like Calm, Insight Timer, Headspace, 10 Percent Happier, and UCLA Mindful or look for directed reflections on YouTube.

5. **Exercise:** Moving your body is one of the most amazing pressure-diminishing exercises. Making time to walk or run outside, bicycle, dance, or practice yoga may be exactly what you want to view as quiet. Every day practice normally delivers pressure diminishing chemicals in your body and works on your by and large actual wellbeing. More on practice benefits.

6. **Put away opportunity for yourself:** Plan time to participate in an action that causes you to feel refreshed or cheerful. It very well may be perusing a book, watching a film, paying attention to music, cleaning up, or strolling your canine around the area.

7. **Watch what you eat and drink:** Picking an eating regimen with entire food sources, including heaps of vegetables, products of the soil grains, is really great for a sound body and brain. Eating admirably and remaining hydrated can likewise assist with settling your temperament. Limit your utilization of profoundly handled food (it's called low quality food on purpose). Additionally shun utilizing liquor.

8. **Spend time in nature:** Concentrates on a show that time in nature decreases pressure. Something as basic as keeping an eye on a nursery

or house plants or strolling through a recreation area can assist with quieting you. (Look into the psychological wellness advantages of nature.)

9. **Ground yourself:** Assuming you're feeling restless, attempt this establishing exercise: respite to name,5 things you can see, 4 things you can contact, 3 things you can hear, 2 things you can smell, and 1 thing you can taste.

Conclusion

As far as some might be concerned, COVID-19 was an endowment of time where they flourished. A sluggish paced, adaptable way of life might have assisted them with zeroing in on themselves or family or work on individual objectives that they lacked the capacity to deal with ahead of time.

Mental medical aid given via prepared local area staff could assist everyone as they with encountering trouble during the COVID-19 pandemic.2 For people suffering aftermath from individual stressors, specialists have prescribed extended utilization of tele wellbeing to distinguish and treat emotional wellness conditions, including despondency, PTSD and other injury related issues, substance use issues, and self-destructive ideation. Self-improvement gatherings, 12-venture projects, otherworldly and strict administrations, vested parties, and representative gatherings telecommuting are all undeniably utilizing intuitive web based stages. Furthermore it is fundamental for social orders to give residents help for occupations, lodging, food, clinical consideration, training, web associations, and numerous other getting through another day needs.

The current global pandemic and conceivably future ones will challenge us and allow us the opportunity to proceed to learn and impart to different countries, ideally connecting us helpfully rather than polarizing us.

CHAPTER SIX

How COVID-19 has altered the natural world's landscape

Introduction

In 2020, numerous nations all over the planet went into lockdown to restrict the spread of COVID-19. The unfortunate news about the developing number of contaminations and passings coming from various pieces of the globe made many individuals significantly decrease their open air action and start socially removing to keep away from disease. Different exercises were likewise advanced by numerous legislatures: the remote work and instruction model was presented for an enormous scope, a few areas of the economy were shut, and remaining at home was suggested. The flare-up of COVID-19 prompts development of the worldwide pandemic, yet there is no particular antibody suggested for COVID-19. In excess of 216 nations are battling against the transmission of the sickness, recuperation and motility. Till date more than 0.948 million passings out of 30.369 million affirmed cases are accounted for by WHO. A large portion of the countries embraced fractional or complete 'lockdown' and forced 'social removing' to control the quick transmission of COVID-19 and its outcome. However worldwide financial development declined because of cross country lockdown, there are sure certain effects on climate. This survey article has talked about the impacts of cross-country lockdown expecting to local area transmission COVID-19 on creature life conduct and barometrical climate in various angles. In the lockdown time frame, the degrees of NO2 and fossil fuel byproduct amazingly decline in air because of limited utilization of petroleum product by ventures, nuclear energy plants and air transportations. The convergence of NO2 dropped by 45-54% in the air of most populated urban areas in Europe. The powers of particulate matters PM2.5 and PM10 diminished by 43% and 31% separately, at lower climate showing improvement in air characteristics in various pieces of world brought about by less traffic and development exercises. SPM diminished up to 15.9%, showing improvement in surface water quality. New abandoned bank has created because of less waterway exercises in this period. Clamor contamination strikingly dipped under 60 db even in packed urban areas. In this manner, the air climate has continued some degree in all regard through such worldwide wide lockdown expecting to control COVID-19 pandemic. The social changes of wild creatures, birds, butterfly, pets and road creatures that pondered biological system of their overall area demonstrate the non-obstruction of human exercises on existences of regular animals during lockdown period. There is sure relationship between's environmental change with the social changes of regular animal during lockdown period.

Flare-up of COVID-19, the greatest pandemic in world (Lu et al. 2020) is probably going to be spread from Huanan Seafood Market, Wuhan, Hubei Province, China. Moving information cost with 30,369,778 affirmed cases, from which 948,795 have kicked the bucket. Covids have a place in enormous family including four genera-α, β, γ and δ infections; yet all strains are not destructive. Among these three strains like SARS-CoV, MERS-CoV and SARS-CoV 19 viewed as more destructive than the others like HCoV-229E, HCoV-OC43, HCoV-NL63 and HCoV-HKUI (Mackay and Arden 2015). Strangely, the strain CoV-19 or SARS-CoV 19 is seen as firmly connected with two bat-determined SARS-like Covid to be specific bat-SL-Cov-ZC45 and bat-SL-Cov-ZXC21 which were confined in 2018 from Zhoushan, China. Genomic examination on Cov-19 has laid out the 79% hereditary comparability with SARS making CoV (SARS-CoV) and half closeness with MERS making CoV (MERS-CoV), affirming that CoV-19 is changed from the over two. So there is banter on the beginning of new CoV-19 is the man made changed or normally transformed strain of Covid (Andersen et al. 2020; Science News 2020).

The rise of another ordinary

The unpredictability incited by the pandemic has sped up numerous business drifts that were pervasive before its spread. Worldwide exchange volume has quickly declined attributable to lockdowns and different other international elements. Associations that depend on lean and without a moment to spare stock chains spread across numerous nations have been especially impacted, because of limitations on the development of work and material. The pandemic has likewise sped up the advanced change, featuring the requirement for solid information as well as fast development. Working in an undeniably unstable worldwide climate expects organizations to fabricate strength and overt repetitiveness and set up their worth chains for future interruptions.

Considering augmenting social incongruities, the job of organizations (especially huge companies and brands) in the general public is being rethought. The emergency has featured the need to twofold down on the SDGs, while centering in the present moment to control the spread of the sickness. Sway has likewise been felt on purchaser conduct, with customers considering brands responsible for a long term benefit. EY's examination shows that reasonableness, wellbeing and supportability are the pivotal issues that brands are to zero in on, assuming they are to really address the requirements of things to come shopper.

The pandemic is probably going to extend calls from different partners for organizations to assume a more dynamic part in tending to cultural difficulties.

Climate, wellbeing and security administrations

The consistence, efficiency and functional issues in overseeing climate, wellbeing and security (EHS) chances have become more extensive and more perplexing. It is currently perceived that overseeing EHS dangers can emphatically affect work environment usefulness and monetary execution.

Maintainable by Design

The signs from the market and from nature are clear: any vision of a recuperation should be maintainable and versatile to successfully answer the difficulties of things to come. This suggests the requirement for organizations to embrace 'Partner Capitalism' and make Environmental, Social and Governance (ESG) a center focal point of their corporate methodology.

EY's Climate Change and Sustainability Services group has fostered a 'Economical by Design' system with a goal to help associations in producing long haul manageable worth by incorporating maintainability standards across the worth chain. This is a three layered structure which empowers the coordination of Environmental, Social and Governance (ESG) standards across the system, activities, and worth chain of the association.

The primary layer relates to the maintainability vision and heading of the business. This requires a complete and centered way to deal with manageability right from the board level through the advancement of administration systems, risk the executives plans and clear targets. The subsequent layer is about execution, which contains the particular functional switches to accomplish those objectives. Execution of ESG drives expects organizations to end a day to day existence cycle perspective on their items and administrations and foster frameworks and cycles that reinforce the ESG execution of the whole worth chain. The third layer relates to the estimation and correspondence of supportability execution. Partners across the range have called for straightforward divulgence of execution information. Organizations might have to systematize hearty measurements and inner administration and control instruments for their ESG information. By lining up with different global divulgence structures, they can bit by bit advance toward better expectations of unveiling long haul esteem. For example, the Embankment Project for Inclusive Capitalism (https://www.epic-value.com/) in which EY is a benefactor, is creating measurements to gauge long haul esteem.

The 'Practical by Design' system is a thorough way to deal with maintainability reconciliation, and an aide than can empower associations to reinforce their establishments and set a direction for an economical and versatile recuperation. The Now, Next and Beyond of the pandemic presents an extraordinary chance for organizations to coordinate the standards of manageability into their methodologies and foster items and administrations that make esteem as per what the earth needs as well as what their partners need. Their job is vital in guaranteeing that the sky in the post COVID world is brilliant and blue.

Natural life and COVID-19

In any case, a significant number of the prompt constructive outcomes of the pandemic on natural life - like diminished street, air, and boat passings or interruption - will probably switch assuming the world returns to the same old thing.

Furthermore, as a rule, it will take ages of progress to assist huge number of species all over the planet with recuperating from the effect of mankind. For instance, it might require 10-15 years of supported decreased fishing to permit the world's drained fish populaces to recuperate.

A few investigations have likewise observed that the pandemic may really be hurting natural life.

In one review, specialists observed that decreased human unsettling influence connecting with lockdown has helped obtrusive outsider species by intruding on the moves that individuals were making to control them. The creators additionally guarantee that pandemic limitations have decreased crafted by preservation and regulation implementation associations that consideration for natural life and safeguarded regions.

Furthermore, this is a worldwide pattern, as the staff of jam, game parks, asylums, and other natural life offices can't play out their typical exercises.

Additionally, the decrease in regulation implementation might cause an unexpected expansion in illicit untamed life killing - specifically, that of imperiled creatures obligated to oppression or poaching.

A few specialists likewise stress that financial difficulty in low pay nations might prompt an expansion in normal asset abuse, for example, unlicensed logging and the illicit natural life market, as individuals run out of ways of making money.

As indicated by satellite pictures, a flood in deforestation is occurring in a few areas of interest. Likewise, illicit fishing rates are on the ascent in Brazil and the Philippines.

The progressions in human action that the pandemic has required may likewise be having a few adverse consequences. For example, a few animal varieties that depend vigorously on people for taking care of or rummaging, like monkeys, gulls, and rodents, might be battling during the pandemic.

Individuals may likewise be utilizing open air spaces, for example, parks and nature saves seriously during lockdown, which could upset occupant untamed life not used to human connections.

On the other side, diminished ecotourism rates are devastating numerous associations worldwide that depend on human guests to take care of and care for their creatures.

In the mean time, plastic contamination from inappropriately discarded single-use COVID-19 defensive stuff additionally is by all accounts expanding the worldwide plastic contamination issue and causing untamed life passings, as creatures can ingest plastic things or become snared or caught in them.

As per one gauge, individuals are discarding as numerous as 3.4 billion single-use facial coverings and face safeguards everyday around the world.

A pandemic of progress?

Numerous analysts and untamed life associations are encouraging researchers and different partners universally to involve this exceptional time for a nearby assessment of the effect of human action on the regular world.

They contend that the data that analysts assemble during this time could assist with further developing preservation and biodiversity endeavors.

It might likewise work on their capacity to anticipate worldwide ecological changes and possible instances of zoonoses, the transmission of sickness from creatures to people. This could save a huge number of living souls, and monetary misfortunes, going ahead.

Everything being equal, it will take more time to survey precisely what the COVID-19 pandemic has meant for untamed life, the climate, and the environment.

Also, the effect of the pandemic on the normal world is probably not going to be straight. Research proposes that a decrease in certain toxins, including nitrogen oxides, may bring about the ascent of others, like ozone.

Seeing how this pandemic has changed people's relationship with nature might be similarly as perplexing.

In any case, for the time being, these positive changes might be to the point of giving certain individuals, and Mother Nature, the expectation of a superior future.

It might likewise assist with enlightening defects in how people communicate with and esteem nature, which could have dependable, extremely durable repercussions for people and the climate the same.

Untamed life and COVID-19: The upside

One significant and predominately sure advantage of the pandemic for untamed life is less human travel.

Because of the critical decrease in ventures, less individuals are hitting and harming or killing untamed life on streets.

A review from March 2021 observed that hedgehog roadkill rates in Poland were over half lower contrasted and pre-pandemic years, saving huge number of hedgehogs in Poland alone. This might assist with switching the drawn out decline of European hedgehog populaces.

Another review dissecting roadkill information from 11 nations observed that roadkill rates fell by over 40% during the initial not many long stretches of the pandemic limitations in Spain, Israel, Estonia, and the Czech Republic.

What's more, less ships are going through the world's streams and seas for transportation, fishing, hydroponics, and the travel industry purposes.

In November 2020, specialists anticipated that worldwide sea exchange would have plunged by 4.1% before that year's over. Different reports assessed a 10% decrease in the holder exchange for 2020.

A decrease in water travel and movement could diminish the gamble of boats striking and harming or killing marine creatures. It might likewise decrease the marine disturbance that happens because of commotion contamination from ships, fishing sonar, and sporting boats.

Birds could likewise be profiting from the sharp decrease in air travel, which might have boundlessly diminished the gamble of bird strikes.

As indicated by the Federal Aviation Administration, somewhere in the range of 1990 and 2019, there were around 227,005 natural life hits with common airplane in the U.S. Also, U.S. planes detailed somewhere in the range of 4,275 additional natural life strikes at unfamiliar air terminals. These strikes brought about injury to 327 individuals.

The pandemic has additionally prompted a declinee in industry supply chains, decreasing interest for business exercises that exploit normal assets in many areas of the planet. For instance, lower fishing interest and movement might lessen the expulsion of creatures from nature.

Furthermore, in India, recounted reports recommend that decreased fishing and vehicle traffic at settling sea shores might be supporting populaces of the fundamentally jeopardized olive ridley ocean turtle.

The pandemic might even help natural life by disturbing the covered up, by and large unlawful inventory chains that annihilate wild populaces, including those that fuel the untamed life exchange.

Going ahead, specialists might begin to take more prompt, strong activity against the illicit abuse and transportation of wild creatures around the world. The World Health Organization (WHO) delivered a report the finish of March proposing that albeit the exact beginning of the pandemic remaining parts tricky, the worldwide natural life exchange might have permitted the infection to enter China.

Analysis and Discussion

"The study features the dire need to check natural life abuse and signals that untamed life exchange might have prompted the pandemic," says Tanya Sanerib, the global legitimate chief at the Center for Biological Diversity.

Coronavirus' impact on creatures

1. Veterinary Activities: Animal government assistance is probably going to be undermined by COVID-19 because of the prompt impacts of the

lockout. Temporarily, during the lockdown, a portion of the veterinary works on with respect to preventive inoculation against previous infections were annulled. Furthermore, the event of contagious animal pre-sicknesses can be brought about by roundabout impacts, for example, expanded untamed life domesticated animals contact, no populace the board or delayed stock on-ranch stays. The drawn out effect of COVID-19 on animal wellbeing would be connected to the financial slump concerning ranchers' vocations and potential for veterinary administrations.

2. Global Wildlife Trade: The pandemic is thought to have arisen in a market in China selling wild creatures, projecting a focus on the worldwide exchange natural life. The Wildlife Conservation Society, situated in New York, is asking policymakers to boycott the market for live creatures and stop the human exchange and carrying of wild creatures. To forestall future pandemics, there are developing calls for nations all over the planet to boycott "wet business sectors" which sell live and dead creatures for human utilization. Elizabeth Maruma Mrema, Acting Executive Secretary of the United Nations Convention on Biological Diversity (UNCBD), and Jinfeng Zhou, Secretary-General of the China Biodiversity Protection and Green Growth Foundation, added their voices to requests for the super durable preclusion of natural life markets by the specialists.

3. Advantage of Quiet Nature Reserves: Very cognizant that poachers might attempt to exploit the lockdown and the absence of development by sightseers in distant regions to complete their criminal operations exceptionally mindful that poachers might attempt to exploit travelers' lockdown and absence of development to do their criminal operations in far off regions. There have been admonitions of an expansion in dealing of imperiled species from Africa to Colombia as guests stay away and many park officers are avoided with regards to work. As per the natural life protection bunch Panthera, there has been an ascent in the poaching of wild felines, including pumas and jaguars, in Colombia, in spite of the fact that there have been bits of gossip about an expansion in tigers being poached in India.

4. Effect on Zoo Animals: As a feature of the public lockdown, zoos all over the planet have been shut and animal specialists gripe that human interest is missing from their most keen and social creatures, including gorillas, otters and meerkats. Nathan Hawke, from the Orana untamed

life park in New Zealand, let The Guardian know that in spite of the way that no one is there to watch them, numerous intriguing and imperiled species kept on turning up for their ordinary "meet the public arrangements.

5. Wildlife is Running Wild: In their homes, with people holing up, creatures that ordinarily stay away from metropolitan conditions currently have opportunity to meander. In northern India, during the cross country COVID-19 lockdown, a crowd of deer was gotten on camera strolling the roads of Haridwar. There has additionally been a significant expansion in the quantity of child Olive Ridley Ocean turtles in India, as sea shores lie void of individuals. Around 60 million eggs are accepted to have been saved for this present year on Indian sea shores.

Coronavirus Factors to improve the Environment.

1. Improved air quality: There are less assembling exercises and less development of vehicles during the lockdown time because of limited homegrown exercises; air contamination diminishes drastically and the environment has continued somewhat. The utilization of petroleum derivatives by industrial facilities, nuclear energy stations, and air transport and vehicle traffic are the significant wellsprings of fossil fuel byproducts. Vehicle traffic has been closed down in the lockdown time for modern areas; the degree of carbon focus is declining.

2. Improved perceivability: Analyzed and kept enhancements in the groupings of seven air pollutants, to be specific particulate matter (PM2.5 and PM10), nitrogen oxides (NOx, NO and NO2), sulfur dioxide (SO2), carbon monoxide (CO) from different populated metropolitan regions in India. PM2.5 diminished drastically across every one of the foreign substances in the majority of the areas. Around 43% lessening in PM2.5 mirrors an abatement in fossil fuel byproducts from limited traffic and a 31% diminishing in PM10 mirror the base re-sedimentation of residue particles brought about by confined work during the lockdown time frame contrasted with the earlier year. Thus, perceivability in various urban areas is a lot higher than it was in the earlier year.

3. Improved nature of water: Water lucidity has incredibly improved and kelp can be imagined in straightforward waters. The lockdown implied cleaning water from the holiest and most dirtied streams of India, The Ganges. In Vembanad Lake, India, upgrades in surface water quality have

been recorded and SPM fixation has diminished by a normal of 15.9 percent contrasted with the earlier year.

4. Less River Activities: Developed Abandoned Banks: all types of waterway transport method for vessels, speedboats, liners, and so forth are restricted during the lockdown time. A specific piece of East Asian individuals are monetarily subject to waterway fishing. For instance, stream tasks drastically quit during the lockdown time frame, bringing about settlement in the waterway bowl.

5. Improved degree of commotion: The sound from airplane, businesses, vehicles, neighborhood amplifiers, occupied markets, and so forth is answerable for some psychological and states of being like dementia, deafness, cerebral pain, stroke, and respiratory failure. One of the principle issues in city life is the humming of the vehicle horns, regularly it arrives at 100 db; commotion contamination has brought down the lockdown for COVID-19.

6. Decreasing interest for oil: Due to the decrease sought after for fuel for production lines and travel, because of the pandemic, there was a sharp lessening of 435,000 barrels each day in the principal quarter of 2020. As one of the main sources of emanations is petroleum derivative ignition, this decline is a decent sign for the climate. Defilement of oil can deliver water unacceptable for water system and damage plants for water system.

7. Declined Global Marine Life Fishing: According to another review, since March 11, when the World Health Organization proclaimed Covid-19 a pandemic, worldwide fishing action has diminished by practically 10% comparative with the 2018-2019 normal, and in certain areas, the downfall has been much more prominent. Supply anchors are divided because of limitations on movement, and fishing imports are diminishing, consequently decreasing deals and affecting fishing networks. Anyway the constructive outcome of the decline in fishing on marine life would rely upon many variables, for example, the life-history attributes of creatures and whether they are reproduced during these months.

Strangely, the reaction of untamed life to changes in the working of human culture and economy was additionally quick. The principal peculiarity saw was that the decrease in human unsettling influence permitted natural life to take advantage of developed environments and to increment everyday activity. Since the start of the pandemic, proof of the presence of wild creature species in regions where they have not been seen for quite a while has been shared via virtual entertainment. Various different changes in creature conduct have additionally been noticed, e.g., in birds' vocalizations during the COVID-19 end ,expanded animosity, changes in taking care of destinations, and the arrangement of new aggressive frameworks in synanthropic species out of nowhere denied of anthropogenic food . During the pandemic, individuals have been offered the chance to acquire unexpected knowledge into what their presence means for creature conduct and how rapidly and deftly creatures can respond to uncommon changes, like lockdown and the "worldwide human control test".

Nonetheless, an inquiry emerges concerning how tireless the current changes in nature will be and what further environmental outcomes they will have on the populaces of wild species. Because of the brief length of this particular anthropause (the World Health Organization announced the pandemic on 11 March 2020), the information showing the effect of the lockdown on key populace boundaries, like overflow, mortality, proliferation, or quality stream, are extremely scanty. More examination is expected to record changes that might influence the crucial attributes of a populace, especially in species with disturbing decreases in numbers. We trust that for such (frequently interesting and secured) species, the lockdown time frame may out of the blue turn into an advanced second in switching negative populace patterns.

What one issue do you think will make the most change for the future of development, and why?

Our future – including our ability to fight pandemics, among other risks – depends largely on our efforts to protect our environment and combat climate change. So, to me, the issue that will best shape how we develop as a society, is the growing *urgency of shifting to a low-carbon economy.*

We have just 10 years left to meet the 2030 Agenda and avert the worst effects of climate change. In many cases, the costs of ignoring the rules of science were laid bare by COVID-19 – and if climate change increases, *the risk of future pandemics increases with it.* Already, heatwaves are melting the permafrost covering the bodies of animals and humans buried by other deadly diseases, such as the plague and anthrax, with anthrax re-emerging in Siberia in recent years. So, as we recover from the COVID-19 pandemic, we must also heed the warnings of our warming world, for greater resilience in the future.

The most effective way to do this is to shift to a new normal which is compatible with the boundaries our planet has set. This calls for ideas, solutions, and models that are both sustainable *and* comprehensive, and facilitate behavioural change across society – from governments to businesses to individuals.

The unprecedented global response to COVID-19 has already proven that this new normal *is* possible. The habits that quickly developed during the pandemic – such as working from home, contact-free services, and reduced travel – demonstrate that we *can* operate under a low-carbon, green model. For the first time in world history, there was even a virtual G20 summit.

With the opportunity to turn greener consumption and operating patterns into our new normal, we should not forget the lessons learned during this crisis or assume that they only apply in a crisis. Rather, we should build upon and mainstream them into government and organisational policies, as well as our behaviour; for instance, by allowing remote working more often to lessen travel emissions. Such changes should also be flanked by further incentives for renewable investments, ensuring a future that is low-carbon, resource efficient, socially inclusive and less vulnerable.

Recommendations

1. Seek to implement current rules for air pollution during and after the COVID-19 crisis.
2. Develop systematic strategies to achieve air quality goals, including through better coordination of land-use planning, transport and environmental policies, through the introduction of economic tools to address emissions from mobile and stationary sources, and through enhanced data collection and quality across monitoring networks.
3. Channel financial support initiatives to boost capacity and efficiency for public transport providers (with focus on reducing crowding and promoting cleaner facilities).
4. Encourage businesses to continue developing cleaner production methods, especially with regard to air pollutant emissions, and to reinforce the use of economic and regulatory instruments to support such innovations.

5. The need to ensure proper ventilation and indoor air quality during containment, especially in winter and wood burning areas, should be clearly communicated. Enable the diffusion of cleaner heating and cooking systems following the COVID-19 crisis in order to boost resistance to potential future epidemics.

6. Secure delivery of safe and efficient water and sanitation facilities to neighborhoods paying particular attention to disadvantaged groups, by for example public fountains and public water taps. Provide detailed statistics on the steps taken to improve water safety.

7. Provide access to hand hygiene stations in all public buildings and transit hubs (either for hand washing with soap or for hand rubbing with alcohol-based rubs).

8. Response and recovery efforts should resolve water affordability problems for households via tailored social interventions (e.g. in the sense of direct household support) and where possible, improve the financial sustainability of utilities that provide critical services.

9. In the longer term, stimulus packages should consider public funding to invest in water-related infrastructure growth and modernisation, leveraging private sector participation where feasible.

10. Systematically screen and exchange pre-treatment information on SARS-CoV-2 in waste water as an early warning system for the health of the linked population and use this information to notify response measures such as community quarantine or enhanced and targeted surveillance.

11. Effective management of biomedical and healthcare waste by adequate identification, processing, separation, storage, transportation, treatment and disposal to ensure that these potentially hazardous waste sources reduce the effects on human health and the environment.

12. Provide instruction and preparation to personnel working in both formal and informal processes of waste collection and management.

13. Maintaining steps of plastic reduction and recycling.

Conclusion

Reports have emerged across the world that the pandemic induced lockdowns have eased some pressure on ecosystems due to the decline in human activity. Improvement in air and water quality and unusual sightings of animals in urban areas have been reported. India, with 6 of the 10 most polluted cities in the world, also witnessed a significant decline in pollution levels since the imposition of the lockdown. For the first time in 30 years, the residents of Jalandhar, Punjab could view the world's tallest mountain range, 200 km away from their city, most likely owing to the reduced pollution levels in the region.

The only preventive measure to regulate population transmission of COVID-19 is the nation-wide lockdown. Clearly due to lockdown steps, global economic growth has decreased, but there are some positive impacts on the atmospheric climate and the sustainable ecosystem. The main contaminants such as nitrogen oxides and carbon have decreased dramatically due to long-term mass containment. In the lower atmosphere and in various parts of the world, increased air quality is caused by fewer traffic and construction activities. The increase in surface water quality is caused by SPM going down to 15.9 percent. At the confluence of the rivers 'Ganga' and 'Yamuna' in India, a very unusual deserted bank is observed to rise in the river basin during lower river activity. Even in crowded areas, noise pollution fell noticeably below 60 db. It can therefore be inferred that by means of such a global lockdown aimed at containing the COVID-19 pandemic, the atmospheric climate has resumed to some degree in all respects. Wild animals, birds, insects, pets and street animals' behavioural changes reflect the interaction of human activities with the lives of natural creatures. There is a certain connection between changes in the environment and the behavioural changes of natural creatures during the time of lockdown. It provides a scope for evaluating the degree of environmental destruction that we are doing in the usual society phase. Finally, though concentrating on conservation here, this is mostly a human disaster, disrupting lives and killing way too many people. The goals of society must be human health and pandemic control, but the resumption of environmental activities and education must also be considered in advance. Here there is a chance to remind people of the relations between good, resilient environments and human well-being.

CHAPTER SEVEN

An Analytical Study of Teenagers' Changing Attitudes During and After Covid-19

Introduction

Coronavirus is the largest form of RNA virus. It causes a respiratory infection that ranges from the common cold to various severe diseases. Today in the whole world coronavirus usually called covid-19 is a crucial topic for every human being. It's a very contagious viral disease that came over in December 2019 and the effects are continuously being spread worldwide. It was foremost discovered in the Wuhan district of China and the World Health Organization on 11th March of the year 2020 acknowledged the severity of the virus and announced it as a source of global pandemic (Corrigan, et. al, 2012). The studies have pointed out that older individuals are very prone to this disease although children have less risk here. But a new form of coronavirus is discovered in the meantime which is causing skin lesions. Children facing routine disruption these days for the closure of schools, colleges, universities. After all these the no of people started suffering from anxiety and psychiatric disorder due to not getting attached with the people during this pandemic situation. (Lee, et. al, 2022). Mostafavi (2021) published a poll in the Michigan Health Blog.

Lockdown made pressure on teenagers not going outside regularly which includes closure of schools and colleges all over the world causing a negative impact on 91% of the world student population. This lockdown system has disrupted the education life, social life, and physical activities too. This has also led to a lack of creativity, innovations, boredom, and not following the routine. The teenagers and children have become more dependent on their parents, clingier, and seeking attention. The cancellation of exams, exchange programs, and academic events has made anxious behaviour for teenagers. It is also found that youth social distancing is a primary way to motivate society to be sincere in their lives. Due to staying at home the use of the internet has increased much more compulsively. Worst of all when the schools and colleges got closed the teenagers and children suffering from household abuse were not able to report violence against this which led to suicides. In India, the student population is 472 million among which 40 million students have a significant effect because they belong to a poor family and are facing inequality in this pandemic situation. They started working in fields, rural areas as servants, and more on. Many teenagers are infected outside their hometown they had to face quarantine separated from their parents and return home. In China this case is performed by several adults, children have been separated from each other and follow the strict quarantine. Every parent got their children in learning and follow the rules given by the governments of the countries particularly. Most of the teenagers were the school students. And during lockdown school students suffered the max. A large number of kids were under depression because they had to drop their schools and were totally clueless about their future. Indian today report explored more about the same.

The pandemic has brought about a complex collection of issues ranging from uncertainty to social isolation, and parental angst that have had an impact on the mental health of children and adolescents. Today's need of teenagers is to be keeping the youth informed and up to date. They also need help teens cope with uncertaintyOffer relief from boredom. One also needs to be focus on athleticsand get youth input to problems and solve them together. There is also a room to address the financial concerns of the younger generations.

One of the most important things to make this feasible is to remember the basics and nature of the virus. "Google's DeepMind" and different AI techs have leaped forward with their knowledge of protein folding research to elucidate the protein morphology of viruses and make it open source.AI technology is being used to create drugs that fight the different hazardous diseases around the world, and when tissues first develop products based on infectious diseases, they are working to further try to treat the coronavirus increase. Within a few weeks of the epidemic, we used our investigative skills to recommend new drugs that could be beneficial. COVID19 is caused by a virus called SARSCoV2. It belongs to the coronavirus family and can range from common head and chest colds to more serious (but rare) illnesses such as "Severe Acute Respiratory Syndrome (SARS) and Middle Eastern Respiratory Syndrome (MERS)" contains a wide range of viruses that cause the disease. .. Like many other respiratory viruses, the coronavirus spreads rapidly through the droplets that erupt from the mouth and nose when breathing, coughing, sneezing, or speaking. COVID19 (Coronavirus Disease 2019) is an illness due to a virus infection called SARSCoV2, which was first identified in Wuhan, China in December 2019. It is highly contagious and is spreading rapidly throughout the world. COVID19 most commonly causes respiratory symbols and can feel like a cold, flu, or pneumonia. COVID19 can attack the lungs and respiratory system, as well as more. Other parts of your body can also be affected by the disease.

Literature Review

The virus has put billions of lives in terrific situations. People are breaking down physically, psychologically, and socially. Compared to SARS COVID has higher transmissibility, worst recovery, frequent mutations leading to uncontrollable situations. This disease not only infects the respiratory system but also goes on damaging the brain, liver, kidneys, and endocrine system with no curable options. There was a lack of emergency treatments has taken away many lives globally.

Most people with COVID-19 have mild symptoms, but some have serious illnesses. Some people, including those with few or no symptoms, may have a post-COVID illness or "long COVID." Elderly people and people with certain underlying illnesses are at increased risk of serious illness due to COVID 19. Hundreds of thousands of people have died of COVID 19 in the United States. Vaccines against COVID 19 are safe and effective. The vaccine teaches the immune system to fight the virus that causes COVID19. Covid-19 has a multi-factorial impact on the children and teenager population, social isolation can trigger, Health policies (Oosterhoff & Palmer, 2020).

The "World Health Organization" has acknowledged coronavirus disease as a pandemic-causing virus in 2019. Global adjustments have been discontinued to prevent the spread of the virus. Pandemics are now defined as situations where a wide range of people are suffering from the same fears, affecting most of the world's population. Symptoms of the coronavirus include respiratory infections, fever and cough, shortness of breath, shortness of breath, tiredness, and sore throat. It also causes new dysphasia, chest compressions, bluish lips, and face. During this pandemic, three groups of people are still at high risk: elderly people over 70 years old, people with chronic illnesses such as diabetes, cancer, high blood pressure, liver disease, cardiovascular disease, and respiratory illness, and physically inactive people (Jiang, et. al, 2021).

Visitors returning home should nod or keep a distance of at least 1 meter and remain in Quarantine for a minimum of 15 days. The family should actually wash their hands while they are together and also disinfect homes, especially places that people often touch. Keep a little distance for those who are not good at staying at home. Seek medical attention immediately if you experience any symptoms. When you are in a public place, follow the same rules as at home. And most importantly, look forward to this situation.

During the situation of covid-19 children and teenagers as well appear to less risked people in this situation. But this pandemic situation has created problems in other ways. The first precaution for these people was to close all the school's high school's colleges and universities all over the world, which lead to being indoors with parents and not seeing close friends and other people. The people who are just crossing the childhood stage to become an adult need proper education and different development needs to be an adult. Now the main factor is social media where teenagers invest their time In a whole day by which they are getting distant from parents. It is a very hard time for a teenager to develop themselves to be good adults (Esposito, et. al, 2022).

Teenagers meanwhile are taught the rules and regulations to be safe and keep the family members safe at the same time. They are said to perform some concrete steps to avoid getting infected, and also not let the loved ones do so. Life has changed so much then the daily routine has also changed widely. Teenagers depend on their mobile phones to connect with their friends and close ones, so the parents need to provide them the facilities rather than simply limiting the use of the internet (Hoffmann, et. al, 2021).

The impact of pandemics on young people is instantly serious. Discuss special things like proms, spending time with friends, going to concerts and more. Now, these things are avoided in this situation leading to distress circumstances, and the results will turn into deeper and long-term consequences. Here it also includes family wellbeing, educational future, and aesthetic participation (Ndulue, & Orji, 2021).

The largest hazard of the coronavirus is the extent of dissemination. Policymakers are introducing measures like quarantines round as a measure to break the chain of spread in the sector due to the fact they can`t thoroughly reveal neighbourhood outbreaks. One of the handiest measures to become aware of sick sufferers thru the observation of CCTV photographs which are nonetheless around us and to discover and separate people who have severe symptoms of the disorder and who've been in contact and sterilized the associated surfaces. Smart device packages are frequently used to preserve an eye fixed on people`s sports and to evaluate whether or not or now no longer they have got are available in contact with an inflamed human. Identification of the infected from the huge population and preventing the transmission of pathogens, they want to expand the reach of vaccinations on a scale to reach herd immunity (Dondi, A., 2021).

According to a study by "the Centres for Disease Control and Prevention (CDC)", teenage suicide attempts increased dramatically during the blockade of Covid 19 in 2020 and 2021. In addition, boys of the same age group also had a 4% increase in suicide attempts. More children were at risk of abuse and negligence at home as the Covid19 or coronavirus pandemic kept children and their families indoors during periods of self-isolation (Lee, et. al, 2021).

People experience a wide multiplicity of new or persistent symptoms that can last for weeks or months after being first infected with the virus that causes COVID19. Unlike other types of post-COVID illnesses of type, which tend to occur only in people with severe illness, those infected with COVID 19 are mildly ill but initially asymptomatic (Zahrin, et. al, 2021).These symptoms can also occur. .. People generally report different combinations of the following symptoms:

Dyspnoea or shortness of breath, fatigue or malaise, symptoms that worsen after physical or mental activity (also known as post-abnormal fatigue), difficulty thinking or concentrating (sometimes called "brain fog"), Cough, chest or abdominal pain, headache, fast heartbeat or throbbing heart (also known as palpitation), joint or muscle pain, pins and needles, diarrhoea, dyspnoea, fever, dizziness when standing up (light-headedness), With skin rashes, mood changes, odour and taste changes, and changes in the menstrual cycle(Jain, et. al, 2020).

Conclusion

There are few ways by which teenagers can be helped in this pandemic situation are: Working together to create a new normal life despite struggling with this situation by sticking to the schedule, conversation time for the home members, and by taking some personal space or we can say it alone time in the home. Communicate honestly and openly with the teenagers and make them understand that it is not the right time to communicate with people outside socially, and share information about what is happening outside the worldwide pandemic. Help them do the plans and recover them from the past situations which can lead to suicidal attempts and can bring mental disorder or disruption. Stay safely connected through the virtual world like Facebook, WhatsApp, whatever the virtual apps are there to make new friend maybe. Bring a sense of responsibility for the family members and help them too to connect with their close ones through the virtual world (Lessard, & Puhl, 2021).

CHAPTER EIGHT

Work-Life Balance Strategies in the Post-Pandemic Era

INTRODUCTION

The word pandemic itself is used to define a phenomenon of global magnitude and thus unwanted to articulate that the Covid-19 Outbreak has impacted each and every sphere of human life. The Pandemic pushed humans into an era similar to the Jurassic world where mankind used to protect themselves by staying inside caves. The human world was drastically put into homes as governments throughout the world announced lockdown to control the spread of viruses. A new culture was introduced in the world of corporates i.e., work from home. Companies are starting to move into the new mode of online working with meetings, work and all the tasks were done on different platforms of the web. Starting from the IT sector to spreading to all different sectors such as research, education, teaching, etc. As the pandemic prolonged both the government and the private companies were looking ways for methods and strategies to reduce the burden of people and provide them with relief. People in general were stressed both financially as well as mentally and the well-being of employees was a matter of concern as it was directly related to efficiency (Saura, et.al, 2022).

The outbreak of COVID-19 has resulted in a slew of unfavorable and dramatic changes in modern corporations' personnel demographics. The COVID-19 virus has evolved into more than a health and financial disaster; it seems to have become a humanitarian catastrophe, especially for those already burdened by fragility, inequality, conflict, and sociopolitical polarization. Respondents with impairments and those who are in risk areas, and those with responsibilities to care for elderly family members, underlined in their remarks the difficult conditions they confront as a result of a failed work-life balance and a lack of assistance. The task for human resource management is to find solutions to reduce the negative consequences of work during the crisis (Pai, et.al, 2021).

Literature Review

The concerns like as global competition, personal life, and a shrinking workforce are causing work-life balance issues. Companies should invest in and monitor these aspects in order to face the difficulties and advance in the global market. Caste system, gender disparity in the workplace, and extensive informal working sectors are all issues that Indians confront when it comes to work-life equilibrium. The author also highlighted some suggested rules and measures that firms could apply in order to boost job satisfaction. Employees have a favorable attitude toward work-life balance and are able to handle both their professional and personal life effortlessly, while the rest are unable to do that for a variety of reasons such as a lack of ambition or a lack of resources (Edwards, & Leigh, 2021).

Employees' well-being has been influenced by factors such as feeling threatened, loneliness, working from home, and insecurity. Managers that need to adapt management techniques to new situations have a big difficulty. In order to operate efficiently, it is also vital to ensure the well-being of employees. Work-life balance is an essential factor that has to be examined and more assistance systems developed. Working from home has resulted in a build-up of professional activities in personal spaces. The physical barrier between the working from the resting area has also been removed. The distinction between the job and the leisure location also became hazy. Time pressures also have altered as a result of the growth of working time at home. As a result, the work-life balance was thrown off, significantly impacting employees' mental health (Habib, 2021).

The confined lifestyle zones theory focuses on the lives in the private light in the work-life equation which is conflicting, although family-related prospect and duties are critical to the category of difficulty that influence outcomes divergence. And though one's private life was hampered by the pandemic, the relations face of the work-life equation become more demanding, elderly parents who had to deal with new demands such as organizing or supervising learning videos for children and managing constant care that had previously been provided by schools or daycare centers (Babapour, et.al, 2022).

Gender bias becomes more relevant as the work shifted from offices to homes. In general, female was burdened with both work as well as with the responsibility of taking care of their children and home. It put a significant amount of pressure on women as they all struggle to strike a balance between the two. The emphasis on infant guidance and protection in the home prompts the study of possibly differing dynamics between men and women. There is a multitude of causes to believe that the countervailing force theory will apply more to women (Laker, & Roulet, 2021). The domestic attachment structure allocates the main duty for home and family to women as an ideal type. The idea of "intense parental care," which also emphasizes women having primary attention to the family sphere and, more particularly, caregiving obligations connected with bringing up a child, is aligned with the domestic love concept. Men, on the other hand, have historically viewed paid employment as the core realm, with their commitment to the "good provider" position exercised in that sphere. Notwithstanding certain cultural improvements, conventional gendered approaches to child care appear to persist, especially in the face of employment limitations. One might anticipate working moms to priorities family-related responsibilities above occupations, especially during a period of increased daycare demands at home, based on this more conventional gendered viewpoint (Mitchell, 2021).

For many employees, societal upheavals during the COVID-19 outbreak reshaped the boundaries between work and nonwork. The investigation of work-home integration as another potential moderator of the countervailing force theory is prompted by this reconfiguring work-home barrier. Even during outbreak, we believe that strong work-home integration will strengthen the opposing influence of children at home (Rajagopal, et.al, 2021).

The justification for all of this viewpoint stems from the description of the employment barrier as a gradient of total segmentation to complete integration under frontier & boundaries explanations. Job gets completed away from the home at a single position when fragmentation is significant; temporal and spatial boundaries represent the hostname's distinctness, with arrangements more akin to the "separate spheres" depiction of work and home roles as having different (often competing) expectations and responsibilities. In contrast, while there is a serious amount of work-home merging, there is minimal differentiation across responsibilities, particularly in terms of the location and time of work- and family-related role enactments (Imam, et.al, 2021).

Parenting and house management becomes a greater problem as employees are locked into their homes with no clear boundary of anything around it. Although the concept of work from home was conceptualized a long time ago it was put into practice during the pandemic. There is a lot of literature on how work from home is done both from employer and employees' perspective. There was hardly any research on how to manage the problems that arise with it. With no boundaries at home as to how work and life to be separated anymore, it added up to the stress of employees (Caligiuri, & De Cieri, 2021). Role-related problems were likely evident for parents striving to get their employment done without offices or venues outside the house to perform their work. Job and family responsibilities were pushed together, with many parents' spouses who were also striving to satisfy work obligations. Furthermore, work's intrusion into the family situation grew more significant as the house became the primary location for teaching children, and disregarding or neglecting children's demands on all aspects risked harming their maturity (Mello, & Grobmeier, 2021).

Parents may have considerable challenges in prioritizing job obligations over their children due to a lack of advice to augment the frequently casual and insufficient enlightening substance presented from school and instructor in the early stages of the pandemic's educational turmoil. Regular reminders that the extended parent role was really being ignored came with doing the task needed of them for compensation. When children were awake, these new and unexpected needs happened on a regular and visceral basis with so few barriers, even in families with plenty of space but when spouses occasionally took leadership. Every ignored inquiry over schooling, every demand for a nibble, and every moment a close relative had to set a miniature kid in front of the television or tape as a "babysitter" may have made parents feel like they were being negligent. Taken together, these characteristics appear to have aided in offsetting the general decline in work-life conflict proportions (Dajani, et. al, 2021).

Another important piece in our research is that the opposing pressure theories need not vary by age. The link between family at home and life & work disagreement, as well as how that relationship altered during the outbreak, did not distinguish both males and females. The relationship appears to contradict the premise that working parents suffered a disproportionately elevated point of life and work conflict amidst the outbreak. Keeping in mind evidence of who has shown gender disparities during the epidemic. The types of job strain encountered by professional women with kids in early months of the deadly disease outbreak may not be reflected by the matter we are applying by means of to quantify it. In an economic meltdown of care, employment which does not produce considerable inter role disagreement (as currently measured) might yet turn out to be necessary to fall. Working that seems to be close to the bottom, piece, but less commended type of occupations which working class women, especially less qualified, tend to just have kicked to the curb first when the teaching and care for children provided by different institutes went

RESEARCH METHODOLOGY:

The present study is descriptive in nature wherein the post pandemic work-life balance strategies was analyzed. The sample taken for the study is 150. The information was gathered with the assistance of an organized poll on a five-point scale and investigated with the assistance of the mean qualities and t test. Demographic profile of the respondents on the post-pandemic work-life balance strategies. There are 49% males and 51% females in the study. Among the respondents 17% are into business, 39% are teachers, 14% are housewives and 30% are students. 34% of the respondents are 20-35 years of age, 37% are 35-50 years of age, and 29% are 50-65 years of age.

The opinions of the respondents is that It is observed The concept of work from home picked up momentum during the pandemic is most significant statement with the mean value of 4.18. It is followed by, Employees who are able to maintain a proper work life balance, have better productivity (4.15), In absence of a proper work life balance, productivity is hampered (4.13), and The work from home concept has diminished the line between work hours and family hours (4.12). There have been massive repercussions post pandemic for every age group (4.10), It is difficult to work from home while the kids are also at home (4.09), It is very important for corporates to consider and work on the issues related to work life balance of their employees (4.08), Work from home concept is way more stressful for women as compared to men (4.07) and Work from home concept has had an adverse effect on the mental status of the employees (4.02) were also considered important. Reasons like Gender bias was another major concern that came to light during the pandemic (4.00) were also viewed as important.

CONCLUSION

There has been a lot of research to suggest that work-from-home life is more stressful for women when compared to men. If one negates the struggle to find the balance between work and life, an increased level of satisfaction is been observed among the employees as it breaks the shackles of corporate structure. Employees now prefer remote working as it saves them from spending a lot of money and tiring commute. Corporate need to fund research to find better strategies for its employees to manage their lives in a new mode, making them productive. Considering analyzing the mentioned research areas inside the framework of the COVID-19 pandemic and the necessity to work remotely, it's important to think about which management strategies can help WLB improve when working from home (Liu, et. al, 2021).

A significant information source for both supervisors and people who work at home is recognizing the most critical factor of assisting employees to achieve WLB and sustaining psychological health when working abroad. Technology is critical in assisting WLB in working remotely situations. Technology can provide a stronger interaction among coworkers as well as improved monitoring of work by supervisors, according to empirical studies on remote working. Increasing WLB among home workers requires ensuring employee socialization via appropriate use of technology. This is especially important since research reveals that during the COVID-19 epidemic, employees feel depersonalized and disconnected. The development of employees' careers is an important subject of WLB study. The chance for workers' growth and training is one of the most important aspects affecting their good view of a business and motivation to report to work. a major impact of e-training on staffer achieving the best result all through COVID-19 (Ramani, 2021).

Bibliography

- Himanshika Sharma, Impact of Make in India over different sectors of India, https://www. businessalligators.com/impact-make-in-india-different-sectors/
- Dr. (Smt.) Rajeshwari M. Shettar, Impact of make in India campaign: A global perspective, http://questjournals.org/jrbm/papers/vol5-issue2/A520106.pdf
- Lee, O., Park, S., Kim, Y., & So, W. Y. (2022, January). Participation in Sports Activities before and after the Outbreak of COVID-19: Analysis of Data from the 2020 Korea National Sports Participation Survey. In *Healthcare* (Vol. 10, No. 1, p. 122). Multidisciplinary Digital Publishing Institute.
- Jiang, R., Shao, B., Si, S., Sato, R., & Tsuneo, J. (2021). Health Communication in Games at the Early Stage of COVID-19 Epidemic: A Grounded Theory Study Based on Plague, Inc. *Games for Health Journal*, *10*(6), 408-419.
- Corrigan, P. W., Morris, S. B., Michaels, P. J., Rafacz, J. D., & Rüsch, N. (2012). Challenging the public stigma of mental illness: a meta-analysis of outcome studies. *Psychiatric Services*, *63*(10), 963-973.
- Dondi, A., Candela, E., Morigi, F., Lenzi, J., Pierantoni, L., & Lanari, M. (2021). Parents' perception of food insecurity and its effects on their children in Italy six months after the COVID-19 pandemic outbreak. *Nutrients*, *13*(1), 121.
- Esposito, C., Di Napoli, I., Agueli, B., Marino, L., Procentese, F., & Arcidiacono, C. (2022). Well-Being and the COVID-19 Pandemic. *European Psychologist*.
- Oosterhoff, B., & Palmer, C. A. (2020). Attitudes and psychological factors associated with news monitoring, social distancing, disinfecting, and hoarding behaviors among US adolescents during the coronavirus disease 2019 pandemic. *JAMA pediatrics*, *174*(12), 1184-1190.
- Hoffmann, A., Nanaki, E., Enevoldsen, P., & Xydis, G. (2021). A behavioral change study in Denmark engaging car drivers in reducing fuel consumption: The key is in the message. *International Journal of Sustainable Transportation*, 1-10.
- Ndulue, C., & Orji, R. (2021, June). Gender and the Effectiveness of

a Persuasive Game for Disease Awareness Targeted at the African Audience. In *Adjunct Proceedings of the 29th ACM Conference on User Modeling, Adaptation and Personalization* (pp. 318-324).

- Lee, J., Lim, H., Allen, J., & Choi, G. (2021). Effects of Learning Attitudes and COVID-19 Risk Perception on Poor Academic Performance among Middle School Students. *Sustainability*, *13*(10), 5541.

- Jain, O., Gupta, M., Satam, S., & Panda, S. (2020). Has the COVID-19 pandemic affected the susceptibility to cyberbullying in India?. *Computers in Human Behavior Reports*, *2*, 100029.

- Lessard, L. M., & Puhl, R. M. (2021). Adolescent academic worries amid COVID-19 and perspectives on pandemic-related changes in teacher and peer relations. *School Psychology*.

- Zahrin, S. N. A., Sawai, R. P., Sawai, J. P., Ab Rahman, Z., & Samsudin, M. Z. (2021). EMOTION, MENTAL AND SPIRITUAL REGULATION OF THE HIGHER EDUCATION COMMUNITY DURING THE COVID-19 PANDEMIC. *ASEAN Journal of Teaching & Learning in Higher Education*, *13*(2).

- Mostafavi (2021) Children's Health, National Poll: Pandemic Negatively Impacted Teens' Mental Health, Michigan Mental Health, March 15, 2021, Retrieved from https://healthblog.uofmhealth.org/childrens-health/national-poll-pandemic-negatively-impacted-teens-mental-health on 22-01-2022, at 10:10.

- Kannan, S. (2020), Covid stress is catching them young, Deep Dive, India Today, Singapore, December 26, 2020, Retrieved from https://www.indiatoday.in/coronavirus-outbreak/story/deep-dive-covid-stress-is-catching-them-young-1753170-2020-12-25   on 22-01-2022, at 10:20.

- https://healthblog.uofmhealth.org/

- Dr.T.V.Ramana, Make in India: Illusion or Possible Reality project?, http://ijar.org.in/ stuff/issues/v2-i2(5)/v2-i2(5)-a002.pdf

- Pratiksha Mishra, Dr.Taruna, Role ofMake in India as a driver of growth in the manufacturing sector, http://www.allresearchjournal.com/archives/2016/vol2issue1/PartI/2-1-76.pdf

- Dr.PuneetAneja, MAKE IN INDIA: New Paradigm for Socio-Economic Growth in India, https://www.worldwidejournals.com/paripex/recent_issues_pdf/2016/ April/April_2016_1460965810 101.pdf

- Major Initiatives, Make In India,http://www.pmindia.gov.in/en/major_initiatives/ make-in-india/ 76 India's Exports and I

- Bordoloi, R., Das, P., & Das, K. (2021). Perception towards online/blended learning at the time of Covid-19 pandemic: an academic analytics in the Indian context. Asian Association of Open Universities Journal.
- Dumford, A. D., & Miller, A. L. (2018). Online learning in higher education: exploring advantages and disadvantages for engagement. Journal of Computing in Higher Education, 30(3), 452-465.
- Jena, P. K. (2020). Impact of Covid-19 on higher education in India. International Journal of Advanced Education and Research (IJAER), 5.
- Keengwe, J., & Kidd, T. T. (2010). Towards best practices in online learning and teaching in higher education. MERLOT Journal of Online Learning and Teaching, 6(2), 533-541.
- Ray, A. E-learning: the new normal in the post-covid world. International Research Journal of Modernization in Engineering Technology and Science, 2(9), 866-876.
- Sruthi, P., & Mukherjee, S. Byju's The Learning App: An Investigative Study On The Transformation From Traditional Learning To Technology Based Personalized Learning. International journal of scientific & technology research, 9.
- Rapanta, C., Botturi, L., Goodyear, P., Guàrdia, L., & Koole, M. (2021). Balancing technology, pedagogy and the new normal: Post-pandemic challenges for higher education. *Postdigital Science and Education*, *3*(3), 715-742.
- Saura, J. R., Ribeiro-Soriano, D., & Saldaña, P. Z. (2022). Exploring the challenges of remote work on Twitter users' sentiments: From digital technology development to a post-pandemic era. *Journal of Business Research*, *142*, 242-254.
- Pai, S., Patil, V., Kamath, R., Mahendra, M., Singhal, D. K., & Bhat, V. (2021). Work-life balance amongst dental professionals during the COVID-19 pandemic—A structural equation modelling approach. *Plos one*, *16*(8), e0256663.
- Habib, M. S. (2021). The need to redefine Work-Life Balance post COVID pandemic in Jordan.
- BabapourChafi, M., Hultberg, A., & Bozic Yams, N. (2022). Post-Pandemic Office Work: Perceived Challenges and Opportunities for a Sustainable Work Environment. *Sustainability*, *14*(1), 294.
- Mitchell, A. (2021). Collaboration technology affordances from virtual collaboration in the time of COVID-19 and post-pandemic strategies.

Information Technology & People.

- Imam, H., Afshan, G., & Samreen, F. (2021). The roles of negative career shocks and work-life balance in depression during pandemic. In *Academy of Management Proceedings* (Vol. 2021, No. 1, p. 12405). Briarcliff Manor, NY 10510: Academy of Management.

- Gigauri, I. (2020). Effects of Covid-19 on Human Resource Management from the Perspective of Digitalization and Work-life-balance. *International Journal of Innovative Technologies in Economy*, (4 (31)).

- Dajani, D., Zaki, M. A., Moustafa, D., & Adel, B. (2021). The Impact of COVID-19 Pandemic on Egyptian Women Psychological Empowerment and Work-Life Balance.

- Ramani, A. (2021). India's transforming post-pandemic workplace: The emerging role of the hybrid work model. *Corporate Real Estate Journal*, *11*(2), 186-192.

- Liu, S., Ren, Y., Li, H., Liu, Y., Shan, J., Yang, L., ... & Chen, H. (2021). Prevention and control strategies for the post-pandemic era: finding a balance between COVID-19 and reviving medical service. *The Journal of Infection in Developing Countries*, *15*(08), 1074-1079.

- Mello, B., &Grobmeier, C. (2021). Teaching Communication in a Pandemic and Post-Pandemic World. *Post-Pandemic Pedagogy: A Paradigm Shift*, 91.

- Edwards, M. S., & Leigh, J. S. (2021). What's the Plan? Some Ideas about JME's Strategy and Preparations for Post-Pandemic Teaching & Learning. *Journal of Management Education*, *45*(4), 523-534.

- Laker, B., & Roulet, T. (2021). How organizations can promote employee wellness, now and post-pandemic. *MIT Sloan Management Review.*

- Rajagopal, K., Mahajan, V., & Ayyagari, K. C. (2021). Human resource management strategies of the Indian information technology sector post-pandemic. In *Handbook of Research on Sustaining SMEs and Entrepreneurial Innovation in the Post-COVID-19 Era* (pp. 191-210). IGI Global.

- Caligiuri, P., & De Cieri, H. (2021). Predictors of employees' preference for working from home post-pandemic. *Business and Economic Research*, *11*(2), 1-9.

- Glantz, E. J., & Gamrat, C. (2020, October). The new post-pandemic normal of college traditions. In *Proceedings of the 21ˢᵗ annual conference on information technology education* (pp. 279-284).

- Fineberg, N. A., Pellegrini, L., Wellsted, D., Hall, N., Corazza, O.,

Giorgetti, V., ... & Laws, K. R. (2021). Facing the "New Normal": How adjusting to the easing of COVID-19 lockdown restrictions exposes mental health inequalities. *Journal of psychiatric research, 141,* 276-286.

- Al Mansoori, M. S., & Ahmad, S. Z. (2021). Adapting to the "new normal" post-pandemic consumer behavior: the case of Rafeeg's strategy of service marketing. *Emerald Emerging Markets Case Studies.*
- Thoreson, C. (2021). Facing A New Normal: Uncovering the Psychological Effects of Loneliness on Student Mental Health.
- Schindler, A. K., Polujanski, S., & Rotthoff, T. (2021). A longitudinal investigation of mental health, perceived learning environment and burdens in a cohort of first-year German medical students' before and during the COVID-19 'new normal'. *BMC Medical Education, 21*(1), 1-11.
- Ghosh, N., & Giri, P. A. (2020). Medical Education During COVID-19 Pandemic–Is Revamping of Existing Curriculum Needed to Adapt to New Normal?. *Annals of Community Health OCT-DEC, 8*(04).
- https://www.oecd.org/coronavirus/policy-responses/strengthening-online-learning-when-schools-are-closed-the-role-of-families-and-teachers-in-supporting-students-during-the-covid-19-crisis-c4ecba6c/
- https://www.weforum.org/agenda/2020/04/coronavirus-education-global-covid19-online-digital-learning/
- http://vikaspedia.in/e-governance/digital-india/digital-india.
- https://www.weforum.org/agenda/2020/08/covid-19-has-accelerated-india-s-digital-reset/
- https://www.outlookindia.com/website/story/outlook-spotlight-how-did-covid-accelerated-digital-transformation-in-india/385365/
- https://www.mckinsey.com/business-functions/strategy-and-corporate-finance/our-insights/how-covid-19-has-pushed-companies-over-the-technology-tipping-point-and-transformed-business-forever
- https://www.indiatoday.in/education-today/featurephilia/story/how-covid-19-is-hastening-the-need-for-education-s-digital-transformation-1708474-2020-08-07
- https://health.economictimes.indiatimes.com/news/pharma/the-pandemic-has-accelerated-our-efforts-towards-achieving-self-reliance-samina-hamied/85810347
- https://hbswk.hbs.edu/item/the-one-good-thing-caused-by-covid-19-innovation
- http://bwsmartcities.businessworld.in/article/How-Tech-Enabled-Smart-Cities-Are-Helping-Fight-Covid19/23-09-2020-323716/

- https://www.financialexpress.com/education-2/covid-19-how-smart-classrooms-are-transforming-indias-education-system/1948670/lite/
- https://www.smartcitiesworld.net/opinions/opinions/how-covid-19-has-made-smart-cities-smarter-than-ever
- https://www.orfonline.org/expert-speak/work-home-anywhere-future-coworking-spaces/
- https://www.indiaglobalbusiness.com/analyses/snap-analysis/smart-cities-indias-potent-weapon-in-the-battle-against-covid-19